A New Theory of Serendipity: Nature, Emergence and Mechanism

Quan-Hoang Vuong (Editor)

The Centre for Interdisciplinary Social Research, Phenikaa University

Yen Nghia, Ha Dong, Hanoi 100803, Vietnam

Title: *A New Theory of Serendipity: Nature, Emergence and Mechanism*

Imprint: Sciendo; part of Walter de Gruyter GmbH

De Gruyter Poland Ltd.
Bogumila Zuga 32a
01-811 Warsaw, Poland
www.sciendo.com

Includes bibliographical references and index.

Cover Illustration: ©2022 Thu-Trang Vuong

ISBN: 978-83-66675-85-8

DOI: https://doi.org/10.2478/9788366675865

Overview

❧ • ❧

The book explores the nature, underlying causes, and the information processing mechanism of serendipity. It proposes that natural or social survival demands drive serendipity, and serendipity is conditional on the environment and the mindset, on both individual and collective levels. From Darwin's evolution theory to Sun Tzu's war tactics, major innovations throughout human history are unified by this key concept. In the rapidly changing world, information is abundant but rather chaotic. The adaptive power of serendipity allows people to notice treasures within this wild sea, but only for those who understand how it works. To increase the probability of encountering and attaining serendipity, one should employ the mindsponge mechanism and the 3D process of creativity, for without these frameworks, serendipity is truly an elusive target. The book also discusses methods to build environments and cultures rich in navigational and useful information to maximize the chance of finding and capitalizing on serendipity. As a skill, serendipity has a resemblance to how kingfishers observe and hunt their prey.

https://doi.org/10.2478/9788366675865-001

Preface

❧ • ❧

Like many curious people, I have long had questions about human creativity, innovativeness, capabilities of creating useful things in life, and sustainability as the most successful animal on this planet we call home.

I cannot say that I have all the answers, but some have been reached along the journey of studying this remarkable capacity of humankind. And this book intends to provide one such answer, specifically about serendipity and its conditions, much linked to the fight for the survival of humankind. Part of the answer arrived when Professor Ngô Bảo Châu – the Vietnamese French mathematician and Fields medalist, currently working at the University of Chicago and serving as Scientific Director of VIASM – told me the critically important period of his research path right before his great accomplishment (see https://en.wikipedia.org/wiki/Ngô_Bảo_Châu) in the 2019 Summer.

The book contains much of my thinking throughout the years of researching and contributions from some affiliates, who serve as contributing authors in several chapters. The book has the appearance of an edited volume. Nonetheless, contribution chapters are not separate; they together form only one answer.

I will show in this book that serendipity is a capacity, first and foremost useful for having creative performance. That capacity is conditional on the environment, the preparatory exercises, and the individual capability of managing information arriving at the individual. In light of this, serendipity is not a myth and is no longer the *thing* solely reserved for geniuses, as we usually think. Everybody can tap this resource for good. As people working in interdisciplinary social

I

https://doi.org/10.2478/9788366675865-002

research, we – the editor and contributing authors – have frequently employed this capacity to complete many of our research works; some of them had been thought of as impossible or unthinkable. That says, we have genuine trust in its value and now want to share it with the readers.

I hope that the book is useful and fun, and thank you for spending your time reading it.

Quan-Hoang Vuong
Hanoi, Vietnam
January 18, 2022
Email: qvuong.ulb@gmail.com

Acknowledgment

❧ • ☙

The editor and contributing authors would like to thank the AISDL research lab at Vuong & Associates (V&A) for providing financial and administrative support. We express our special thanks to Dam Thi Thu Ha, V&A's Director, artists Vuong Thu Trang and Bui Quang Khiem.

The editor thanks his long-term research collaborator, Professor Nancy K. Napier (Boise State University, Idaho, USA), for her joint effort in developing some key concepts employed in this volume, such as "serendipity as a strategic advantage", "mindsponge", and "3D multi-filtering processes." These concepts serve as the cornerstones of the subsequent academic discussions presented in this volume.

https://doi.org/10.2478/9788366675865-003

Table of Contents

https://doi.org/10.2478/9788366675865-toc

About the Editor and Contributors

Quan-Hoang Vuong (Ph.D., Université Libre de Bruxelles) is Director of the Centre for Interdisciplinary Social Research (Centre ISR) and Distinguished Scientist of Phenikaa University, Hanoi, Vietnam. He is the Founding Chair of the Vietnam Chapter of the European Association of Science Editors. Dr. Vuong serves in the NAFOSTED Scientific Council on Basic Research in the Social Sciences and Humanities (2019–2022) and as a Distinguished Associate Member with Vietnam Institute for Advanced Study in Mathematics (VIASM, 2021-2024). He has published more than 200 academic papers and books with such publishers as Brill, De Gruyter, Elsevier, Emerald, Inderscience, MIT Press, Nature Publishing Group, Oxford University Press, Palgrave Macmillan, SAGE, Springer, Taylor & Francis, Warwick University Press, Wiley, World Scientific, etc. Dr. Vuong is also active as an editor and reviewer, helping handle hundreds of manuscripts submitted to numerous journals. His analytical views have been widely shared on such news outlets as AFP, AseanAffairs, ETF Trend, Forbes, La Città Futura, La Reppublica, Los Angeles Times, New York Times, Roubini Global Economics, Sina.com, Stratfor, Wall Street Journal, etc.

Minh-Hoang Nguyen holds an MSc in Sustainability Science from Ritsumeikan Asia Pacific University, Beppu, Japan, where he continues his Ph.D. track. He works as a researcher in the Centre for Interdisciplinary Social Research, Phenikaa University, Hanoi, Vietnam. Mr. Nguyen has published more than 40 research articles in journals by multiple publishers: Cell Press, De Gruyter, Elsevier, Emerald, MDPI, MIT Press, Nature Research, Oxford University Press, Springer, and Wiley. Besides research articles, he has also co-authored two books about statistical analysis methods and psychology. His research interest is about psychological issues. He believes

https://doi.org/10.2478/9788366675865-004

understanding human mental constructs and mechanisms through the lens of information processing is a fundamental approach for achieving sustainability in multiple disciplines.

Tam-Tri Le holds an MSc in Sustainability Science from Ritsumeikan Asia Pacific University, Beppu, Japan. Currently, he is working as a researcher in the Centre for Interdisciplinary Social Research, Phenikaa University, Hanoi, Vietnam. He has published more than ten research articles and books on mental health, scientific publishing, and business. His research interests are metaphysics and general psychology. He believes that many psychological phenomena can be studied by examining the perception of value and the fundamental mechanism of belief.

Quy Van Khuc is currently a lecturer at the Faculty of Political Economy, University of Economics and Business, Vietnam National University. He holds a bachelor's degree in Social Forestry from the Vietnam National University of Forestry. He obtains a master's degree in Environmental and Resource Economics, a doctorate in Forest Sciences at Colorado State University (Fort Collins, USA). Before returning to Vietnam, he spent a year as a Postdoctoral fellow at the Department of Geography, University of Alabama (Tuscaloosa, USA). Dr. Khuc has published in top-tier journals such as *Humanities and Social Sciences Communications*, *Forest Policy and Economics*, *Ecology and Society*, *Environmental Research Letters*, etc. He focuses on three major areas: culture, environment, and innovation.

Viet-Phuong La is a researcher at the Centre for Interdisciplinary Social Research, Phenikaa University, Hanoi, Vietnam, and a software engineer for A.I. for Social Data Lab, Vuong & Associates, Vietnam. He has published around 40 peer-reviewed articles in multiple journals. He has also edited a book about the statistical analysis of social data. His specialty is software engineering and statistics.

List of Figures

https://doi.org/10.2478/9788366675865-005

List of Tables

https://doi.org/10.2478/9788366675865-006

Chapter 1:
A question lingering for ten years

Quan-Hoang Vuong

ॐ • ॐ

This chapter provides the context and reasons for the new theory of serendipity proposed in this book. This is an investigation into the nature, cause, and mechanism of serendipity. The book's content is structured based on the theoretical development flow, and the book structure is presented at the end of the chapter.

ॐ • ॐ

1.1. Humankind development and serendipity

Human history is a history of innovation. Many important inventions that shaped our civilization were built upon seemingly random discoveries. But without these major "coincidences", The human society we see today would have been very different - that is, if we were lucky enough to survive this far. The modern human species (*Homo sapiens*) only appeared several hundred thousand years ago, which can be considered extremely "young" compared to many species currently existing on Earth. Existential threats to humans have always been there, sometimes direct, sometimes lurking, but our survival as a species is never ensured. In the primitive age, human existence was constantly threatened by predators, food shortages, diseases, and internal conflicts. While our modern civilization has successfully lowered the impacts of these existential threats, the danger will never be completely eliminated. There will always be a

https://doi.org/10.2478/9788366675865-007

possibility that an individual would die due to unwanted causes, and similarly, there will always be risks of our species ceasing to exist. In fact, we are likely to be already in a mass extinction event on Earth, where the human species is the major driving factor (Kolbert, 2014).

On the instinct of fighting for survival, humans aim to become stronger – in the sense of being "fitter". The idea of "survival of the fittest" in human social contexts was popularized by the 19th-century philosopher Herbert Spencer (Spencer, 2020) in close relation to the foundational theory of natural selection originated from the famous naturalist Charles Darwin's work (Darwin, 2003). Many other species on Earth far out-lived humans. In the comparatively "short" duration of human existence so far, we struggled with some serious existential threats and came quite close to extinction, such as during the recent ice age, the Cold War period, or the incoming possible environmental catastrophe. Jared Diamond discussed the fall of human society on the two main causes of environmental destruction and internal conflicts (Diamond, 2011). The survival instinct that keeps humanity alive also drives people to war between different groups, as seen from our history of intraspecific conflicts (Von Clausewitz, 2008). War has been a big factor in the advancement of civilizations as a strong drive for innovation (Lee, 2016; Satia, 2019).

Whether being against external or internal existential threats, it is our survival desire that makes us strive for "strengths" – whatever forms it may take: knowledge, technology, military and political power, or social well-being and cooperation.

Under environmental and social stress, the ability to notice potentially valuable information in one's surroundings can be considered a skill that significantly increases one's advantages in the struggle for existence. Serendipity has been under many major breakthroughs in humankind's advancement. The direct battlefront of natural survival started with our ancestors a very long time ago. From observing natural fire randomly encountered and realizing its values, early humans tried to create and control fire, which gave the population an immense leap in power against the cold, the dark, dangerous predators, and much more (Gowlett, 2016). Regarding food and diet, human ancestors started by collecting so many random items they found in the environment. Over time, they selected edible, nutritious, and cultivable things – typically, grain as staple foods (Choi, 2016). The ability to quickly notice good sources of nutrition might have also led to the discoveries of some foods we are familiar with today, such as cheese, yogurt, and coffee. The same patterns can be seen in early tool making as well as in modern medical breakthroughs. The Covid-19 pandemic is a serious crisis for human society (Schell et al., 2020). As a typical example in our current age, the rapid development of vaccines against the threat of the Covid-19 pandemic has considerably benefitted from serendipity (Vuong et al., 2022).

The desire for knowledge, technology, and influence drove science, art, and business inventions on the battlefront of social survival. Serendipity was present in many popular stories, from Newton's apple, Archimedes' bathtub to Picasso's paintings and Solvay's ammonia-soda process. Striving for competitive advantages among groups and countries also fuels wars across eras (Von Clausewitz, 2008). The ability to notice useful information on the battlegrounds is crucial in wars, as seen through the formulation of strategies in the famous ancient military book "The Art of War" (孫子兵法) by Sun Tzu (孫子) – one of the earliest strategists to document and summarize war tactics and theories (Tzu, 2021).

The human strength we have today has been built on countless innovations. Humankind has come this far, and as serendipity is a major factor in innovation (Fink et al., 2017), we need to ask ourselves if humans really got those wonderful inventions out of pure luck, or is serendipity conditional on something else. Still, we have yet been aware of its mechanism. After all, mysterious phenomena are those not being well-understood. Now it is time to take off the mystery veil covering the miracles of serendipity.

1.2. A ten-year question

In life, there are a lot of coincidences. But coincidences do not happen completely by chance, but certain conditions are required. One special type of coincidence holding enormous potential values is the so-called "serendipity". There have been a considerable number of scientific inquiries on the concept of serendipity. I started a research project on serendipity in 2011, ten years before I wrote the current lines. This, too, can be seen as a typical case of the recently proposed and promoted "slow science movement" (Alleva, 2006; Stengers & Muecke, 2018).

Nancy K. Napier (Boise State University, Idaho, US) and I began a conceptual development study more than ten years ago. In 2013, the study was published in the form of a book chapter (Napier & Vuong, 2013). Serendipity is a highly abstract concept, and it used to be a rarely used term in the English language before the 21st century. And upon usage, we often pair it with synonyms like "luck" or "fate", generally indicating something happening accidentally or unexpectedly. Following this notion, we perceive the concept of serendipity as something out of our control, intention, or even consciousness.

But this is not the concept of serendipity in my mind. This is also not the kind of concept that is helpful in our approach to knowledge. We need something that is well-definable, applicable, and can be solidly based on to continue developing theories or practices further. From the beginning, despite the slight differences in interpretation between Nancy and me, we both pictured serendipity as a powerful tool in humans' mental planning processes. The reason for this orientation was that we focused on the operating systems of finance and management at the time. Thus, the initial title was "Serendipity as a competitive advantage" and later adjusted to be more comprehensive as "Serendipity as a strategic advantage?".

While the study could be considered a valuable contribution based on the positive responses from my colleagues as well as observations on its applications in other studies, I personally still have a big lingering question about the nature of serendipity. I have realized the limitation of this study. Similar to many other studies on "how to make good use of resources", it fails to answer the questions about the essence (properties), the root (causes), and the formation mechanism of serendipity. In other words, the question – "what are the nature, the causes, and the mechanism leading to serendipity moments?" – was left largely unanswered. This is a deadly limitation, for it obstructs deeper development of the theory for benefiting human society and activities (including business and science).

My question on the nature of serendipity did not appear after the article was published, but it had appeared long before I even started writing the manuscript. However, with the study's aims and the length limit with only a 20-page frame, the question was not prioritized to be answered. And so, the question has been lingering in my mind for ten years. Although I have been quite busy with other research projects, this question has never gone away, but it kept growing instead. Why is this still the case even though the article was already published and its values have been well recognized?

After time and time again, I received the benefits of serendipity, and the signs of those serendipitous events have been obvious. The strategic advantages it brought are also undeniable (Vuong, 2018). Year by year, the urge to understand its meaning and mechanism (the "nuts and bolts" of serendipity) became more and more provoking. I soon deemed the pursuit of the answer to this question a debt for myself. Furthermore, thanks to the positive observable results and the clues from published papers, the ability to trace and connect hidden factors within serendipity phenomena were also improved (Vuong, 2021a, 2021b).

At this moment, having figured out the answer that more or less fulfilled my ten-year aspiration, I will now write it down with colleagues to complete my quest. The answer will surprise many, even those working in academia, management, and psychology. I could find out this answer by applying the theories of mindsponge and 3D creativity processes (Vuong, 2016; Vuong & Napier, 2014, 2015) – which are, interestingly, two theories being born with the helping hand of serendipity.

1.3. Structure of the book

The content of the book is structured as follows.

Chapter 1: [A question lingering for ten years] Showing the reasons for a new theory of serendipity and introducing the book's content.

Chapter 2: [How do we perceive serendipity?] Reviewing past literature on serendipity's definitions, types, influential factors, and processes with support from bibliometric analysis.

Chapter 3: [A conditional process to serendipity] Proposing and discussing the conditionality of serendipity.

Chapter 4: [Serendipity as a survival skill] Proposing and discussing the underlying survival motives of serendipity as well as its nature as a skill for such survival purposes.

Chapter 5: [Natural and social survival: the drivers of serendipity] Exploring deeper the two types of survival drivers for serendipity: natural and social survival.

Chapter 6: [A new theory of serendipity] Presenting a new theory of serendipity by integrating all major points presented in preceding chapters.

Chapter 7: [Conditions improving serendipity encounter and attainment probability] Providing models describing scenarios with different degrees of serendipity success probability and discussing corresponding conditions.

Chapter 8: [From soul-touching concept to serendipity greatness] Explaining the concept and how the "soul factor" contributes to the serendipity outcomes.

Chapter 9: [Revisiting the floppy-eared-rabbit serendipity circumstance] Explaining the floppy-eared-rabbit case of serendipity by applying the new theory.

Chapter 10: [Environments and cultures that nurture serendipity strikes] Discussing how to build an environment rich in both navigational and useful information for supporting serendipity.

Chapter 11: [Preliminary explanations of serendipity based on non-linear information process] Presenting a preliminary attempt to explore the information process of serendipity further using a non-linear approach.

Chapter 12: [Reflecting on the new theory of serendipity] Summarizing the book content and reflecting on the applicability of the serendipity-mindsponge-3D (SM3D) framework.

Chapter references

Alleva, L. (2006). Taking time to savor the rewards of slow science. *Nature, 443*(7109), 271-271.

Choi, C. (2016). Ancient Chinese may have cultivated grass seeds 30,000 years ago. *PNAS Journal Club.* https://blog.pnas.org/2016/03/journal-club-ancient-chinese-may-have-cultivated-grass-seeds-30000-years-ago/

Darwin, C. (2003). *On the origin of species* (D. Knight, Ed. Reprint ed.). Routledge.

Diamond, J. M. (2011). *Collapse: how societies choose to fail or survive.* Penguin Books.

Fink, T. M. A., Reeves, M., Palma, R., & Farr, R. S. (2017). Serendipity and strategy in rapid innovation. *Nature Communications, 8,* 2002.

Gowlett, J. A. J. (2016). The discovery of fire by humans: a long and convoluted process. *Philosophical Transactions of the Royal Society B: Biological Sciences, 371*(1696).

Kolbert, E. (2014). *The sixth extinction: an unnatural history* (First edition). Henry Holt and Company.

Lee, W. E. (2016). *Waging war: conflict, culture, and innovation in world history.* Oxford University Press.

Napier, N., & Vuong, Q. H. (2013). Serendipity as a strategic advantage? In T. Wilkinson (Ed.), *Strategic management in the 21st century* (pp. 175-199). Praeger/ABC-Clio.

Satia, P. (2019). *Empire of guns: the violent making of the Industrial Revolution.* Stanford University Press.

Schell, D., Wang, M., & Huynh, T. L. D. (2020). This time is indeed different: A study on global market reactions to public health crisis. *Journal of Behavioral and Experimental Finance, 27*, 100349.

Spencer, H. (2020). *The principles of biology: Volume 1*. Outlook Verlag.

Stengers, I., & Muecke, S. (2018). *Another science is possible: A manifesto for slow science*. John Wiley & Sons.

Tzu, S. (2021). *The art of war*. Vintage.

Von Clausewitz, C. (2008). *On war*. Princeton University Press.

Vuong, Q. H., & Napier, N. K. (2014). Making creativity: the value of multiple filters in the innovation process. *International Journal of Transitions and Innovation Systems, 3*(4), 294-327.

Vuong, Q. H., & Napier, N. K. (2015). Acculturation and global mindsponge: An emerging market perspective. *International Journal of Intercultural Relations, 49*, 354-367.

Vuong, Q.-H. (2016). Global mindset as the integration of emerging socio-cultural values through mindsponge processes: A transition economy perspective. In J. Kuada (Ed.), *Global mindsets: exploration and perspectives* (pp. 109-126). Routledge.

Vuong, Q.-H. (2018). The (ir)rational consideration of the cost of science in transition economies. *Nature Human Behaviour, 2*, 5.

Vuong, Q.-H. (2021a). The semiconducting principle of monetary and environmental values exchange. *Economics and Business Letters, 10*(3), 284-290.

Vuong, Q.-H. (2021b). Western monopoly of climate science is creating an eco-deficit culture. *Economy, Land & Climate Insight*. https://elc-insight.org/western-monopoly-of-climate-science-is-creating-an-eco-deficit-culture/

Vuong, Q.-H., Le, T.-T., La, V.-P., Nguyen, T. T. H., Ho, M.-T., Khuc, Q., & Nguyen, M.-H. (2022). Covid-19 vaccines production and societal immunization under the serendipity-mindsponge-3D knowledge management theory and conceptual framework. *Humanities and Social Sciences Communications, 9,* 22.

Kingfisher

©2017 Bui Quang Khiem

Chapter 2:
How do we perceive serendipity?

Quy Khuc

❧ • ☙

In order to set a ground for the new hypotheses, theory, and conceptual framework of serendipity, the current chapter aims to review the research landscapes, definitions, types, influential factors, and processes of serendipity. First, bibliometric analyses of 2982 documents retrieved from the Web of Science database were employed to examine the intellectual and conceptual structures in the research field of serendipity. Three major research lines are found: 1) information-seeking behaviors, 2) serendipity in business and sciences, and 3) serendipity in recommender systems. Then, a narrative review of the most notable documents and studies was done to overview the serendipity's definitions, types, influential factors, and processes. Based on the review, we stipulate the literature gap in which the newly proposed hypotheses, theory, and conceptual framework will fit in.

❧ • ☙

2.1. Overall landscapes of serendipity research

Before delving into the newly proposed theory and conceptual framework, reviewing the research landscapes, definitions, types, influential factors, and processes of serendipity is worthwhile. The bibliometric techniques were initially employed to reveal major themes and the development in the field of serendipity research. Specifically, the intellectual and conceptual structures were examined

https://doi.org/10.2478/9788366675865-008

using VOSviewer, a bibliometric software for visualizing scientific landscapes (Van Eck & Waltman, 2014). The intellectual structure represents major research lines and their intellectual origins, while the conceptual structure expresses the conceptual focuses and their temporal change within the studied topic (Nguyen, Nguyen, et al., 2021). Here, we performed co-citation – the frequency of two documents being cited together by other units – analysis to explore serendipity research's intellectual structure (Zupic & Čater, 2015). The conceptual structure was investigated by analyzing keyword co-occurrences (that is, keywords appear in the same document) (Nguyen, Pham, et al., 2021). The analyzed documents were retrieved from the Web of Science database (WoS) on December 14, 2021, using the following search query: TS = ("serendipity").

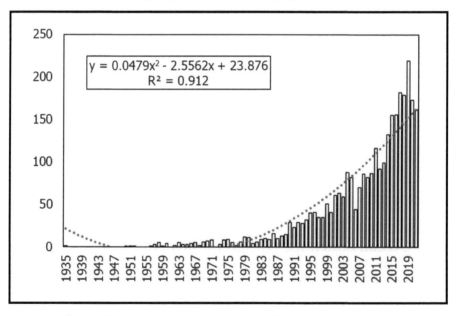

$$y = 0.0479x^2 - 2.5562x + 23.876$$
$$R^2 = 0.912$$

Figure 2.1: Annual publications related to serendipity

The search resulted in 2982 documents in total. Five document types with the highest number of publications are research article (1615 documents), proceeding article (459), editorial material (276), review article (236), and book chapter (120), respectively. The first WoS-indexed publication about serendipity was the discussion of Rosenau (1935) on the concept of serendipity in 1935. Before the 1990s, only 55 serendipity-related documents were published, accounting for less than 2% of the total publications. Nevertheless, the annual number of publications on serendipity has grown exponentially since then (see Figure 2.1).

A co-citation analysis was performed using a threshold of minimum citation number of the cited reference at 20, so 46 cited documents with a minimum of 20 citations are visualized in Figure 2.2 using fractional counting. Fractional counting was selected due to its theoretical and empirical advantages over full counting (Perianes-Rodriguez et al., 2016). Three features have to be considered when interpreting the intellectual structure map:

- The node's size is proportionate to its citation;
- The distance between nodes represents the frequency of being co-cited; and,
- The node's color denotes the major research line.

The co-citation analysis on the cited references of 2982 documents shows three major research lines within the research field dedicated to serendipity as follows.

1) *Information-seeking behaviors* (red),
2) *Serendipity in business and sciences* (blue), and
3) *Serendipity in recommender systems* (green)

Table 2.1: Ten most influential publications

Author	Publication title	Publication type	Local citations*	Research line
Foster and Ford (2003)	Serendipity and Information Seeking: An Empirical Study	Research article	105	1
Merton and Barber (2004)	The Travels and Adventures of Serendipity: A Study in Sociological Semantics and the Sociology of Science	Book	99	2
Andel (1994)	Anatomy of the Unsought Finding. Serendipity: Origin, History, Domains, Traditions, Appearances, Patterns and Programmability	Research article	84	2
Roberts (1989)	Serendipity: Accidental Discoveries in Science	Book	80	2

Herlocker et al. (2004)	Evaluating collaborative filtering recommender systems	Research article	61	3
Makri and Blandford (2012)	Coming across information serendipitously – Part 1: A process model	Research article	58	1
Ge et al. (2010)	Beyond accuracy: evaluating recommender systems by coverage and serendipity	Proceeding article	57	3
Kotkov et al. (2016)	A survey of serendipity in recommender systems	Review article	56	3
McBirnie (2008)	Seeking serendipity: the paradox of control	Review article	51	1
Cunha et al. (2010)	On serendipity and organizing	Review article	44	2

* Local citation is the number of times a reference is cited by the generated pool of documents (2982 documents)

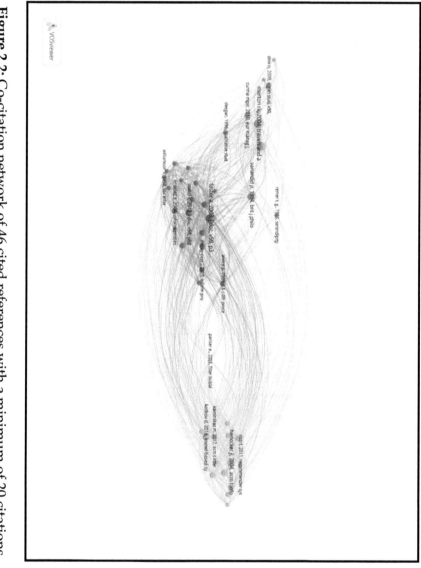

Figure 2.2: Co-citation network of 46 cited references with a minimum of 20 citations (fractional counting)

Studies in the first research line – so-called *serendipity and information-seeking behaviors* – mainly investigate the notion of serendipity in information-seeking contexts. In detail, they study how to increase the probability of obtaining serendipity which is usually considered to be "fortuitous" in nature (Foster & Ford, 2003; Makri & Blandford, 2012; McBirnie, 2008). The most influential research in this line is the study of Foster and Ford (2003) about the nature of serendipity in information-seeking behaviors of interdisciplinary scholars (see Table 2.1). Inquiring how to improve the chance of encountering serendipity in the digital environment is a recently emerging topic in this research line (Makri et al., 2014; Rubin et al., 2011).

The distance from the first to the second research line – named *serendipity in businesses and sciences* – is relatively proximate. This is because the focal topics in the second research line are mostly about the roles of serendipity in businesses and sciences (Cunha et al., 2010; Dew, 2009; Eisenhardt, 1989; Fine & Deegan, 1996; Yaqub, 2018). The most cited works in this research line include two well-known books about serendipity: *The Travels and Adventures of Serendipity: A Study in Sociological Semantics and the Sociology of Science* written by Merton and Barber (2004) and *Serendipity: Accidental Discoveries in Science* written by Roberts (1989). Distinct from the first and second research lines, which tend to look at the psychological and behavioral aspects leading to serendipitous moments, the third research line – named *serendipity in recommender systems* – is technology-intensive. Serendipity is one of the two main quality evaluation metrics of a recommender system, so exploring how to improve serendipity in recommender systems is the primary aim of this research line. In the recommender system context, serendipity is associated with "the novelty of recommendations and in how far recommendations may positively surprise users" (Ge et al., 2010).

We performed a co-word analysis employing a threshold of the minimum number of keyword occurrences at 20, which generates a conceptual map of 41 most frequently occurring keywords (see Figure 2.3). Both Author Keyword and Keyword Plus were included in the analysis. The ten most frequently occurring keywords in serendipity-related studies are model (79 occurrences), innovation (53), design (52), creativity (47), recommender systems (47), behavior (45), discovery (44), seeking (42), expression (37), and information (36). These keywords are closely aligned with three main research lines identified using co-citation analysis.

The conceptual map in Figure 2.3 illustrates not only the occurrence of each keyword (proportionate to the node size) but also the temporal order of each keyword, in accordance with the node's color. Explicitly, the more yellow the node is, the more recent the corresponding concept of the given node emerges. The ten most recently emerging concepts are literature listing (average publication year of 2018.48), recommender systems (2017.23), life (2016.45), search (2016), information-seeking (2015.04), stability (2014.87), drug discovery (2014.45), performance (2014.25), plates (2013.84), and cancer (2013.83). Literature listing keyword indicates a new type of publications that aims to introduce a list of newly published books, journal and conference articles on patents related to life sciences and pharmaceuticals, software, patent policy, strategic issues, and trademarks, etc. (Bates, 2017, 2019, 2020). The lists are partly generated by "serendipity."

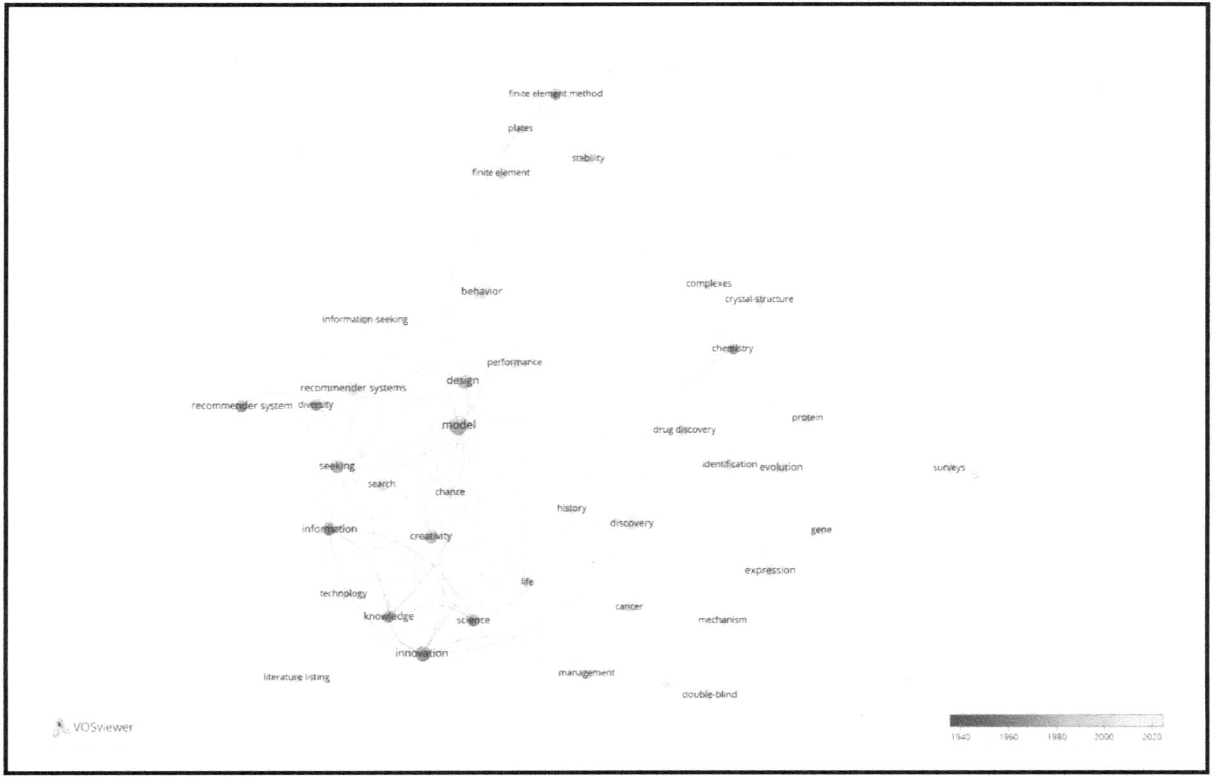

Figure 2.3: Temporal co-word map of 41 keywords with a minimum of 20 occurrences (fractional counting)

Moreover, the serendipity-related topics about recommender systems and information-seeking behaviors are quite new. Despite the fact that serendipity has long been occupying a crucial position in scientific progress, the relationship between serendipity and pharmaceutical and medical discoveries has been attracting more attention from scientists quite lately (Curtin, 2020; Ekins et al., 2017; Grivtsova et al., 2021; Sampat, 2012; Stahl & Baier, 2015).

From these keywords, it can be seen that the serendipity concept is in most cases linked with progressive concepts (e.g., innovation, creativity, and discovery), information-seeking behaviors, and recommender system operation. In the next sub-sections, we will delve into the definitions, typology, influential factors and processes of serendipity.

2.2. Definitions and types

- **Definitions**

The word "serendipity" was coined by Horace Walpole, an English novelist and the youngest son of British Prime Minister Robert Walpole, in a letter that he wrote to his distant relative, Horace Mann. The word originated from the term "Serendip" in the fairy-tale *"The Travels and Adventures of Three Princes of Serendip,"* which was about three princes who discovered things they were not looking for by accidents and sagacity on their adventures. The three princes in the story are sons of Jafer, king of Serendip. Serendip is the Old Persian name for Sri Lanka nowadays (Merton & Barber, 2004).

Despite appearing centuries ago, the term "serendipity" has only become fashionable, and its concept has been systematically studied by scientists quite recently. By 1958, the word had appeared in print solely 135 times (De Rond, 2014). However, a straight Google search today (as of December 26, 2021) can result in more than 30 million websites containing references to serendipity, while a quick search in Google Scholar generates around 168 thousand results.

The definition of "serendipity" is various and usually refers to chance, fate, luck, destiny, karma, coincidence, providence, etc. (Sethna, 2017). According to Merton and Barber (2004), Horace Walpole – the word's inventor – regarded serendipity as "[…] making discoveries, by accidents and sagacity, of things which they were not in quest of […]." The Cambridge Dictionary defines it as "the fact of finding interesting or valuable things by chance." Other researchers define serendipity as an accidental or unexpected discovery of something that turns out to be valuable (Cunha et al., 2010). For instance, Denrell et al. (2003) refer to serendipity as "not just luck, but effort and luck joined by alertness and flexibility," while Andel (1994) thinks of it as "the art of making an unsought finding."

Such unexpectedness is derived from "the anomalous event, the unanticipated result, the idiosyncratic outlier, the incongruous finding, the chance conversation", as Brown (2005) depicted. Seizing anomalous data or taking advantage of unexpected phenomena can sometimes result in accidental discoveries. Merton (1948) refers to this pattern as serendipity. In other words, serendipity pattern is a "fairly common experience of observing an unanticipated, anomalous and strategic datum which becomes the occasion for developing a new theory or for extending an existing theory", he elucidates. If the unexpected information, events, or opportunities are successfully capitalized and turned into serendipitous discoveries, they can generate innovation and strategic advantage for not only the individual but also the organization or science (Copeland, 2019; Napier & Vuong, 2013; Vuong, 2018).

Taking advantage of unexpected information or data anomalous with existing thought, findings or theories is beneficial but not simple. It requires the alertness, preparedness, and capability to notice what others do not, recognize, consider, and connect disparate pieces of information or find opportunities. Like Louis Pasteur famously remarked, *"Dans les champs de l'observation le hasard ne favorise que les esprits prepares"* [In the fields of observation, chance favors only prepared minds]. Without a prepared mind, which is well-stocked with relevant knowledge, a person is not able to identify remarkable events or pieces of information from the background and insignificant occurrences (Charlton & Walston, 2002).

De Rond (2014) describes serendipity as a capability to identify and connect disparate observations, events, or fragments of information into "matching pairs" that lead to surprisingly effective results. This capability is analogous to Albert Einstein's combinatory play, which is "the act of opening up one mental channel by dabbling in another" (Gilbert, 2016). Nevertheless, other researchers advocate that serendipitous discoveries require both luck and skill to happen and are both unpredictable and can be cultivated (André et al., 2009; Copeland, 2019). In particular, serendipity is "the finding of unexpected information (relevant to the goal or not) while engaged in any information activity" and "the making of an intellectual leap of understanding with that information to arrive at an insight", as stated by André et al. (2009). Thus, serendipity is not simply blindly stumbling on important phenomena or simple trials and waiting for the luck to come, but it requires highly insightful questions and searching for solutions (Thagard & Croft, 1999).

From the definitions mentioned above, it can be seen that serendipity holds four typical characteristics. First, serendipitous moments occur in the context that unsought, unexpected, unanticipated, and unintentional phenomena or *'datums'* (or pieces of information) are found. Second, such phenomena and datums are anomalous, out-of-ordinary, surprising, and inconsistent with existing thoughts, findings, or theories. Third, it requires alertness, preparedness, or capability to recognize and capitalize on unexpected, anomalous phenomena and datums for attaining serendipitous moments (e.g., adding values, developing or expanding theories, discoveries). Finally, the successfully attained serendipitous moments will generate strategic advantages for multiple levels (e.g., individual, organization, and social levels).

- **Typology**

In extending Merton's (1968) serendipity pattern, Fine and Deegan (1996) concentrate on the chance aspects and analytically classify serendipity into three types: 1) *temporal serendipity,* 2) *serendipity relations,* and 3) *analytic serendipity. Temporal serendipity* is the moment a person creates a classic ethnography from mundane materials when being exposed to a specific dramatic event "in the right place at the right time." The *serendipity relations* indicate the "unplanned building of social networks" that provide more valuable knowledge or lead to new connections. The last category – *analytic serendipity* – features the ability to link between data and theories, which in turn generate useful and valuable insights.

Napier and Vuong (2013) propose another typology of serendipity, which is based on previous works of Foster and Ford (2003), Cunha et al. (2010), Roberts (1989), and De Rond (2014). They categorize serendipity based on two factors: 1) whether there is an explicit intention to find something and 2) whether unexpected information solves an existing problem or reveals solutions to unknown problems. The categorization displayed in the 2-2 matrix diagram leads to three types of serendipity (see Figure 2.4). Type 1 illustrates the situation in which a person wants to solve problem A, but the solution comes from unexpected information or event B that they did not intentionally look for. Type 2 is the circumstance that a person looks for a solution to A, but information or event B emerges and leads to solutions to C. Type 3 describes the case that a person does not explicitly intend to look for anything but finds information or event B that helps solve problems C and D.

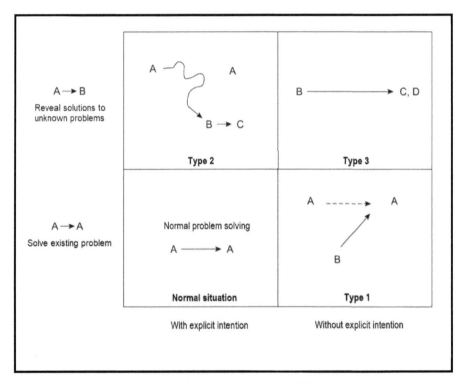

Figure 2.4: Three types of serendipity. Modified from Napier and Vuong (2013) and De Rond (2014).

In a recent taxonomy study, Yaqub (2018) categorizes serendipity into four types: 1) *Mertonian serendipity*, 2) *Walpolian serendipity*, 3) *Bushian serendipity*, and 4) *Stephanian serendipity*. The classification is based on two questions: "what type of solution did the discovery lead to?" and "is there a targeted line of inquiry?" Despite some distinctions, the classifications of Fine and Deegan (1996), Napier and Vuong (2013), De Rond (2014), and Yaqub (2018) emphasize the association between unexpectedness and problem-solving.

2.3. Influential factors and processes

Even though the serendipity moment is unexpected, many scientists advocate that serendipity can be cultivated in *specific* environments and through *certain* personal traits and skills. Cultural, digital, and physical environments are vital in increasing the chance of encountering the necessary pieces of information that can lead to serendipity moments. Particularly, in a culture that endorses risk-taking, withholding of blame, and openness to new ideas and discussion, people are more likely to interact and share knowledge with each other, which in turn enhances the likelihood of facing unexpected valuable information or events (Cunha et al., 2010; Mendonça et al., 2008). Moreover, when a culture can tolerate a degree of autonomy for experiments, "controlled sloppiness", and minimal structure, it will also help stimulate serendipity (De Rond, 2014; Dew, 2009; Mendonça et al., 2008).

Apart from the cultural environment, digital and physical environments holding "trigger-rich", "highlights triggers", "enables connections", and "enables capturing" factors are also able to facilitate serendipity processes (McCay-Peet & Toms, 2015). In an experimental study of 47 digital users, Toms (2000) finds that suggestion tools can direct users to some useful newspapers and increase serendipitous encounters. Zhang et al. (2012) suggest that the *Auralist* recommendation system can enhance serendipity among users listening to music while balancing it with other conflicting goals, like accuracy, diversity, and novelty. Additionally, the availability and design of physical spaces (e.g., sewing club, public library) for social connections, information sharing, cross contacts, diversity, pointers, imperfections, and *'explorability'* also affect serendipity (Björneborn, 2008; Pálsdóttir, 2011).

Regarding personal traits and skills, McCay-Peet and Toms (2015) advocate that openness, prepared mind, and abilities to make connections are three significant factors that can improve the chance of experiencing serendipity. To elaborate, openness is a personal trait, conscious strategy, or temporary state representing a person's receptiveness to experience; the prepared mind is referred to a person's knowledge and experience; connection-making abilities indicate a person's critical and creative thinking about the relationship between encountered ideas, information, and events and their existing knowledge and experience. Williams et al. (1998) and Andel (1994) also share similar opinions about the effects of openness and prepared mind on serendipity processes. For being able to see and pursue serendipitous events, the following traits and skills are also necessary:

1) gaining motivations to work hard and perform well;
2) capitalizing on social networks effectively;
3) being willing to take risks; and,
4) attaining a good "grip on reality" (Delcourt, 2003; Dew, 2009; Diaz de Chumaceiro, 2004; Gaglio & Katz, 2001).

Some scientists also propose models illustrating the process of serendipity. One of the first models is the model of organizational serendipity suggested by Cunha (2005). He separates the serendipity process into four sequential blocks. The first block represents a set of precipitating conditions that can increase serendipitous discovery (e.g., temporal happenstance, active learning, and relational or social networks). The second block is the search for solutions for a certain problem. The third block is named *'bisociation'*, meaning the combination of unrelated skills, information, or events when looking for solutions for the given problem. This bisociation leads to the unexpected finding of a solution for a particular problem (the fourth block). Adapting the model of Cunha (2005), McCay-Peet and Toms (2010) develop a model of the serendipity process in the context of knowledge work. The model introduces "observation of a trigger" as a new component standing for external stimuli or important elements of surprise (e.g., text, images, audio).

Also, based on Cunha (2005)'s model of the serendipity process, Makri and Blandford (2012) delve into the process, from *making a new connection* (the connection is known as bisociation) to *serendipity*. They suggest that the serendipity process begins when "a new connection is made between an informational or non-informational need and a "thing" (e.g., person, event, place, information, object) with the potential to address the need." Then, the potential value of the connection is projected. If the connection is considered valuable, it will be exploited and reflected. Simultaneously, backward-facing reflections are also made on the circumstances' unexpectedness leading to the connection-making. The experience can be deemed serendipity after reflecting on both the outcome values and the involvement of unexpectedness.

Lawley and Tompkins (2011) think that a perceptual process of serendipity comprises of six components:

1) *a prepared mind,*

2) *an unplanned or unexpected event,*
3) *recognizing the potential for serendipity,*
4) *seizing the moment,*
5) *amplifying the confluence of consequences,* and
6) *evaluating the effects.*

Analogous to Lawley and Tompkins's (2011) thinking, Rubin et al. (2011) also emphasize the importance of a prepared mind and the ability to notice the potential of an unexpected event or information. They propose a conceptual framework with five components:

1) *the find,*
2) *prepared mind,*
3) *act of noticing,*
4) *chance,* and
5) *the fortuitous outcome.*

The find is the essence of what is encountered by chance. Serendipitous encounter is accidental and only available to a person with a prepared mind (prior concerns and previous experiences) and the ability to notice it.

Recently, McCay-Peet and Toms (2015) consolidated the aforementioned models into a single model of the serendipity process. The model has five major elements:

1) *trigger,*
2) *connection* (and possible delay),
3) *follow-up,*
4) *valuable outcome,*
5) *unexpected thread,* and
6) *perception of serendipity.*

Trigger is the catalyst for serendipity, which can be verbal, textual, or visual. *Connection* is the recognition of a relationship between a trigger and existing knowledge or experience. The recognition does not always happen immediately so it can be delayed, which is similar to the incubation period of McCay-Peet and Toms (2010). *Follow-up* represents actions taken to capitalize the *connection* and generate a valuable outcome. *Valuable outcome* is the positive effect of the serendipitous experience. *Unexpected thread* is an unexpected, accidental, or surprising element that is evident in at least one of the previous elements. *Perception of serendipity* is an experience "understood or regarded to be serendipitous based on awareness of its *trigger, connection, valuable outcome,* and *unexpected thread*" (McCay-Peet & Toms, 2015).

In general, many researchers have striven to define the definition, typology, and processes leading to serendipity moments, but the answers to the question of where serendipity comes from remain largely unclear. Previous studies have pointed out that serendipity emerges from a bisociation (or a connection between a trigger and existing knowledge or experience) and how to increase the chance of encountering such a connection and the ability to exploit it. Moreover, they also emphasize the unexpected nature of what McCay-Peet and Toms (2015) define as an *unexpected thread* during the serendipity process. Nevertheless, we propose that the process leading to serendipity is a conditional process rather than unexpected or accidental. Serendipity is a humans' survival skill not only in nature but also in social contexts. The next chapters of the book will be dedicated to clarifying our hypotheses, theory and conceptual frameworks using the mindsponge mechanism (Vuong & Napier, 2015; Vuong, 2016) and the 3D information process of creativity (Vuong et al., 2022; Vuong & Napier, 2014).

Chapter references

Andel, P. (1994). Anatomy of the unsought finding. Serendipity: origin, history, domains, traditions, appearances, patterns and programmability. *The British Journal for the Philosophy of Science, 45*(2), 631-648.

André, P., Schraefel, M., Teevan, J., & Dumais, S. T. (2009). Discovery is never by chance: designing for (un) serendipity. *Proceedings of the Seventh ACM Conference on Creativity and Cognition,* 305-314.

Bates, S. (2017). Literature Listing. *World Patent Information, 48,* 29-41.

Bates, S. (2019). Literature Listing. *World Patent Information, 57,* 41-54.

Bates, S. (2020). Literature Listing. *World Patent Information, 61,* 101963.

Björneborn, L. (2008). Serendipity dimensions and users' information behaviour in the physical library interface. *Information Research, 13*(4), 370.

Brown, S. (2005). Science, serendipity and the contemporary marketing condition. *European Journal of Marketing, 39*(11/12), 1229-1234.

Charlton, B. G., & Walston, F. (2002). Individual case studies in clinical research. *Journal of Evaluation in Clinical Practice, 4*(2), 147-155.

Copeland, S. (2019). On serendipity in science: discovery at the intersection of chance and wisdom. *Synthese, 196*(6), 2385-2406.

Cunha, M. P. (2005). Serendipity: Why some organizations are luckier than others. *FEUNL Working Paper Series,* 472.

Cunha, M. P. e., Clegg, S. R., & Mendonça, S. (2010). On serendipity and organizing. *European Management Journal, 28*(5), 319-330.

Curtin, N. J. (2020). The development of Rucaparib/Rubraca®: A story of the synergy between science and serendipity. *Cancers, 12*(3), 564.

De Rond, M. (2014). The structure of serendipity. *Culture and Organization, 20*(5), 342-358.

Delcourt, M. A. (2003). Five ingredients for success: Two case studies of advocacy at the state level. *Gifted Child Quarterly, 47*(1), 26-37.

Denrell, J., Fang, C., & Winter, S. G. (2003). The economics of strategic opportunity. *Strategic Management Journal, 24*(10), 977-990.

Dew, N. (2009). Serendipity in entrepreneurship. *Organization Studies, 30*(7), 735-753.

Diaz de Chumaceiro, C. L. (2004). Serendipity and pseudoserendipity in career paths of successful women: Orchestra conductors. *Creativity Research Journal, 16*(2-3), 345-356.

Eisenhardt, K. M. (1989). Building theories from case study research. *Academy of Management Review, 14*(4), 532-550.

Ekins, S., Diaz, N., Chung, J., Mathews, P., & McMurtray, A. (2017). Enabling anyone to translate clinically relevant ideas to therapies. *Pharmaceutical Research, 34*(1), 1-6.

Fine, G. A., & Deegan, J. G. (1996). Three principles of Serendip: insight, chance, and discovery in qualitative research. *International Journal of Qualitative Studies in Education, 9*(4), 434-447.

Foster, A., & Ford, N. (2003). Serendipity and information seeking: an empirical study. *Journal of Documentation, 59*(3), 321-340.

Gaglio, C. M., & Katz, J. A. (2001). The psychological basis of opportunity identification: Entrepreneurial alertness. *Small Business Economics, 16*(2), 95-111.

Ge, M., Delgado-Battenfeld, C., & Jannach, D. (2010). Beyond accuracy: evaluating recommender systems by coverage and serendipity. *Proceedings of the Fourth ACM Conference on Recommender Systems*, 257-260.

Gilbert, E. (2016). *Big Magic: Creative Living Beyond Fear*. Riverhead Books.

Grivtsova, L. Y., Falaleeva, N. A., & Tupitsyn, N. N. (2021). Azoximer Bromide: mystery, serendipity, and promise. *Frontiers in Oncology*, *11*, 699546.

Herlocker, J. L., Konstan, J. A., Terveen, L. G., & Riedl, J. T. (2004). Evaluating collaborative filtering recommender systems. *ACM Transactions on Information Systems*, *22*(1), 5-53.

Kotkov, D., Wang, S., & Veijalainen, J. (2016). A survey of serendipity in recommender systems. *Knowledge-based Systems*, *111*, 180-192.

Lawley, J., & Tompkins, P. (2011). *Maximising serendipity: The art of recognising and fostering unexpected potential - A systemic approach to change*. The Clean Collection. https://cleanlanguage.co.uk/articles/articles/224/1/Maximising-Serendipity/Page1.html

Makri, S., & Blandford, A. (2012). Coming across information serendipitously–Part 1: a process model. *Journal of Documentation*, *68*(5), 684-705.

Makri, S., Blandford, A., Woods, M., Sharples, S., & Maxwell, D. (2014). "Making my own luck": serendipity strategies and how to support them in digital information environments. *Journal of the Association for Information Science and Technology*, *65*(11), 2179-2194.

McBirnie, A. (2008). Seeking serendipity: the paradox of control. *Aslib Proceedings*, *60*(6), 600-618.

McCay-Peet, L., & Toms, E. G. (2010). The process of serendipity in knowledge work. *Proceedings of the Third Symposium on Information Interaction in Context, 377–382*.

McCay-Peet, L., & Toms, E. G. (2015). Investigating serendipity: how it unfolds and what may influence it. *Journal of the Association for Information Science and Technology, 66*(7), 1463-1476.

Mendonça, S., Cunha, M., & Clegg, S. R. (2008). Unsought innovation: serendipity in organizations. Entrepreneurship and Innovation—Organizations, Institutions, Systems and Regions Conference, Copenhagen.

Merton, R. K. (1948). The bearing of empirical research upon the development of social theory. *American Sociological Review, 13*(5), 505-515.

Merton, R. K. (1968). *Social theory and social structure*. Free Press.

Merton, R. K., & Barber, E. (2004). *The travels and adventures of serendipity: a study in sociological semantics and the sociology of science*. Princeton University Press.

Napier, N., & Vuong, Q. H. (2013). Serendipity as a strategic advantage? In T. Wilkinson (Ed.), *Strategic management in the 21st century* (pp. 175-199). Praeger/ABC-Clio.

Nguyen, M.-H., Nguyen, H. T. T., Le, T.-T., Luong, A.-P., & Vuong, Q.-H. (2021). Gender issues in family business research: A bibliometric scoping review. *Journal of Asian Business and Economic Studies*. (Ahead-of-print).

Nguyen, M.-H., Pham, T.-H., Ho, M.-T., Nguyen, H. T. T., & Vuong, Q.-H. (2021). On the social and conceptual structure of the 50-year research landscape in entrepreneurial finance. *SN Business & Economics, 1*, 2.

Pálsdóttir, Á. (2011). Opportunistic discovery of information by elderly Icelanders and their relatives. *Information Research, 16*(3), 485.

Perianes-Rodriguez, A., Waltman, L., & Van Eck, N. J. (2016). Constructing bibliometric networks: A comparison between full and fractional counting. *Journal of Informetrics, 10*(4), 1178-1195.

Roberts, R. M. (1989). *Serendipity: Accidental Discoveries in Science.* Wiley.

Rosenau, M. J. (1935). Serendipity. *Journal of Bacteriology, 29*(2), 91-98.

Rubin, V. L., Burkell, J., & Quan-Haase, A. (2011). Facets of serendipity in everyday chance encounters: a grounded theory approach to blog analysis. *Information Research, 16*(3), 488.

Sampat, B. N. (2012). Mission-oriented biomedical research at the NIH. *Research Policy, 41*(10), 1729-1741.

Sethna, Z. (2017). Editorial. *Journal of Research in Marketing and Entrepreneurship, 19*(2), 201-206.

Stahl, M., & Baier, S. (2015). How many molecules does it take to tell a story? Case studies, language, and an epistemic view of medicinal chemistry. *ChemMedChem, 10*(6), 949-956.

Thagard, P., & Croft, D. (1999). Scientific discovery and technological innovation: Ulcers, dinosaur extinction, and the programming language JAVA. In L. Magnani, N. J. Nersessian, & P. Thagard (Eds.), *Model-based Reasoning in Scientific Discovery* (pp. 125-137). Kluwer Academic.

Toms, E. G. (2000). Understanding and facilitating the browsing of electronic text. *International Journal of Human-Computer Studies, 52*(3), 423-452.

Van Eck, N. J., & Waltman, L. (2014). Visualizing bibliometric networks. In *Measuring scholarly impact* (pp. 285-320). Springer.

Vuong, Q. H. (2016). Global mindset as the integration of emerging socio-cultural values through mindsponge processes: A transition economy perspective. In J. Kuada (Ed.), *Global mindsets: exploration and perspectives* (pp. 109-126). Routledge.

Vuong, Q.-H. (2018). The (ir)rational consideration of the cost of science in transition economies. *Nature Human Behaviour, 2,* 5.

Vuong, Q. H., & Napier, N. K. (2014). Making creativity: the value of multiple filters in the innovation process. *International Journal of Transitions and Innovation Systems, 3*(4), 294-327.

Vuong, Q.-H., & Napier, N. K. (2015). Acculturation and global mindsponge: an emerging market perspective. *International Journal of Intercultural Relations, 49,* 354-367.

Vuong, Q.-H., Le, T.-T., La, V.-P., Nguyen, T. T. H., Ho, M.-T., Khuc, Q., & Nguyen, M.-H. (2022). Covid-19 vaccines production and societal immunization under the serendipity-mindsponge-3D knowledge management theory and conceptual framework. *Humanities and Social Sciences Communications, 9,* 22.

Williams, E. N., Soeprapto, E., Like, K., Touradji, P., Hess, S., & Hill, C. E. (1998). Perceptions of serendipity: Career paths of prominent academic women in counseling psychology. *Journal of Counseling Psychology, 45*(4), 379.

Yaqub, O. (2018). Serendipity: Towards a taxonomy and a theory. *Research Policy, 47*(1), 169-179.

Zhang, Y. C., Séaghdha, D. Ó., Quercia, D., & Jambor, T. (2012). Auralist: introducing serendipity into music recommendation.

Proceedings of the Fifth ACM International Conference on Web Search and Data Mining, 13-22.

Zupic, I., & Čater, T. (2015). Bibliometric methods in management and organization. *Organizational Research Methods, 18*(3), 429-472.

Kingfisher

©2017 Bui Quang Khiem

Chapter 3:
A conditional process to serendipity

Quan-Hoang Vuong

---

୧ • ୨

This chapter proposes that the occurrence of serendipity is not purely based on chance but conditional, despite the unexpectedness upon noticing and realizing the value of the "missing piece" information. A serendipity phenomenon requires many different conditions to be satisfied, including the environment and the current mindset. One needs to ask the right questions and have the right tools to pursue their answers.

୧ • ୨

3.1. The personal take on serendipity

Regarding the nature of serendipity, while the phenomenon is perceived as unexpected, accidental, or surprising by the experiencing person, I see it as a conditional occurrence. Based on my personal experiences, I will illustrate this specific notion.

In 2018, my family and I spent the summer in Dijon, France – where our daughter was studying. My wife and I usually went to the MonoPrix supermarket located in the central shopping district in the morning. We often passed through a little park named Jardin Darcy on the way there. One morning out for a walk, I heard some faint sounds of birds. I told my wife that the sounds must have come from some

https://doi.org/10.2478/9788366675865-009

baby birds. Jardin Darcy had a lot of birds at the time, but I knew those were the distinct sounds of wild birds. Anyway, it was really hard to locate exactly where the sounds came from.

On the way home, passing through the same place, we could not hear them anymore. But then suddenly, a large bird flew out of the bush. It looked like a dark-colored starling but a bit bigger. I guessed it might have been a mother bird. It was getting dark then, so we decided to go home.

The next morning, I decided to go to that location again to check for the bird nest. This time, I still heard the chirping of baby birds. Probably the day before, they did not make noise when the mother bird brought back something to feed them. But that morning, they were getting hungry again and became noisy little guys. I found my way into the bushes and heard them louder, but there was no nest in sight.

Upon careful looking at a branch attachment about eye level, there was a big bag surrounded by trash. Thinking that could be the only place for the nest, I slightly pull down the branch. And there, just as expected, I found four day-old-chick beaks open wide, waiting to be fed. Probably they sensed my movements nearby and thought their mother returned with food. Some of these little hatchlings had yet to be able to open their eyes.

For me, the event of finding the bird's nest is very exciting and memorable. This positive feeling is not from the coincidence, but it has a very deep reason. This reason points to the mechanism underneath the emergence of a serendipity moment. I will return to discuss this later; for now, let us continue with the story.

After discovering the nest, I took some pictures and recorded a short video of those baby birds (see Figure 3.1).

Figure 3.1: Day-old chicks with their hungry mouths in Darcy, taken on July 11, 2018.

The nest was made from materials found around Jardin Darcy, including things like trash, plastic bags, strings, and even cigarette butts – the last one is an important detail. Several weeks later, I read an article in the journal *Science* about how some animals, such as birds, know how to use toxic materials to make nests for preventing attacks. I recalled the image of those cigarette butts that usually carry a repulsive odor. Again, I was surprised about the value of keeping useful information even when its usefulness has not been carefully assessed. This is the core principle of the serendipity concept that Nancy and I set up in our research (Napier & Vuong, 2013).

But the story continued. In the late summer of 2018, I was in Hanoi when the city's suburban areas were suffering from heavy floods. The impacts of Hanoi's flooding at the time were reported quite severely in both local and international news. One day, sitting at a café by the road with some colleagues, I heard the chirps of baby birds. That was strange because I knew for sure there were no bird nests around that place. Looking closely, I found three baby birds too young to fly properly. They were only able to hop around a corner. A small plastic pipe released wastewater from an air conditioner about five or six meters above the ground on the wall. The birds were jumping around that corner of the wall, taking turns drinking the wastewater.

This scene is striking (see Figure 3.2).

I took a picture using my old cellphone from a six- or seven-meter distance (I was afraid they might run away if I got closer). The image created a juxtaposition in my mind. At a time when there were flooded areas within the city, these birds had to drink wastewater coming from an air conditioner!

This was a very important insight that helped me investigate the issue of ecological inequality, which led to the birth of the semiconducting principle of monetary and environmental values exchange (Vuong, 2021a).

It was used first in my keynote address and conference paper presented at the ASEAN Conference for Young Scientists on December 2, 2019, at Phenikaa University. A year later, the speech's content was published as an article in the *Journal of Sustainability Education* (Q.-H. Vuong, 2020), in which the picture of the baby birds drinking an air conditioner's wastewater holds a special position, appearing early in the paper with a careful explanation on its origin and meaning.

However, a hidden factor was not included: the image of the bird's nest I found in Darcy Park.

Figure 3.2: Baby birds drinking wastewater, taken on August 10, 2018.

It was used first in my keynote address and conference paper presented at the ASEAN Conference for Young Scientists on December 2, 2019, at Phenikaa University. A year later, the speech's content was published as an article in the *Journal of Sustainability Education* (Q.-H. Vuong, 2020), in which the picture of the baby birds drinking an air conditioner's wastewater holds a special position, appearing early in the paper with a careful explanation on its origin and meaning. However, a hidden factor was not included: the image of the bird's nest I found in Darcy Park.

These studies reflect my thoughts on the environment and how such thoughts are connected to my interactions with nature, based on the serendipity mechanism of collecting and quick-assessing information's values. But the flow continued. In November 2021, at the same time, Vietnam Prime Minister Pham Minh Chinh gave his statements in the fight against climate change at COP26 alongside other country leaders (Thanh, 2021), another article where I directly addressed the global-scale inequality in climate science was published on the *Economy, Land & Climate Insight* (ELCI, the platform has received support from the European Climate Foundation) (Vuong, 2021b).

These successful projects have their origins related to pieces of information initially deemed as almost insignificant, as the notion of serendipity suggests. However, they emerged following a workflow with a mechanism similar to what we see in scientific research activities. While the connections between events seem vague and hidden, they are not loose and weak but rather very solid and logical.

It can be seen through the concise statements in my mentioned ELCI article (Vuong, 2021b), which reflects a connection throughout many completed research projects (see four publications listed in the paper's reference section). Here I want to emphasize the systematicity: the process becoming complete thanks to the final missing pieces – such as the birds' nest in Jardin Darcy or the birds drinking the air conditioner's wastewater. Serendipity is indeed the keyword.

However, this book does not focus on making use of the value of serendipity but on explaining the source or origin from which serendipity emerges. And thus, we will explore why the property of conditionality is so important.

3.2. The importance of conditionality

To begin with, I would like to clarify that while the images and sounds of baby birds are valuable to me based on my cultural value system and scope of interest, they can be of very little value to another person. Each person has a distinct mindset (a set of core values) that helps attach value to and assess the obtained information from the environment. This notion is stipulated in the mindsponge information-processing mechanism (Vuong, 2016; Vuong & Napier, 2015). Therefore, one's perceived value (or the degree of importance) of information depends on the individual's mindset (Nguyen et al., 2021; Nguyen & Vuong, 2021).

This is a key point. Only when the tendency to highly value a particular piece of information exists in a person's mindset would the probability of receiving and accepting that information increase. Otherwise, there is a high chance that such pieces are quickly rejected or discarded when a lot of information keeps flowing in. In my case of receiving the information of the bird sounds in Darcy, the subjective assessment was based on a long personal history of nurturing the values of birds in relation to my living environments.

Autumn 1977, I had just started to take my first classes in a public school for a few days. There were often a lot of images (e.g., fruits, animals, vehicles) in reading exercises to make it easier for children to recognize objects and spell words. An interesting incident happened. The teacher asked a guy in my class named Hưng to spell a word in a picture. As he was not paying attention, he read the wrong one in a proud and loud voice: "Ma'am, it's a bird nest!"

Everyone who paid attention in the class knew that this guy got the question wrong on three levels. First, it was not the right picture but a different one below. Second, it was supposed to be a single word –

"nest" rather than "bird's nest". Third, he was supposed to spell the word instead of saying what the picture was about. For us children, it was really fun to see someone making mistakes on so many levels. As a result, besides being punished for his inattention, the guy also gained the nickname: "Hưng the Bird-nest".

The incident left a big impression on my mind. Looking at the beautiful illustration in the textbook, I also noticed that the nest was made skillfully, and the baby birds inside were cute and lively. But as a child living in Hanoi, a capital city, it was not easy to see a real bird's nest, so my desire to see a natural bird's nest kept growing over time. I saw birds flying around and singing on trees now and then but was never able to find a nest, let alone watching baby birds with their hungry mouths like in Jardin Darcy in 2018 (see Figure 3.1).

After some time, back in the late 1970s, a friend in my apartment complex picked up a baby sparrow somewhere and showed me. At the time, I knew a little bit about sparrows' color and natural habitats. But my friend gave me an important hidden fact: the sides of a baby sparrow's beak have two yellow stripes. In the eyes of a child, I found it to be a marvelous piece of knowledge. Indeed, when the bird grew up to a certain point, the yellow stripes disappeared, leaving only the dark-brown color. I also observed a "miracle": when my friend whistled, the bird flew out and landed on his arm. The notion of a bird landing on one's arm or shoulder just from a whistle seemed wondrous. I also tried to whistle several times, but the bird did not come to me. I really admired this guy so much for his "power of controlling" wild birds. Sadly, later he told me that the bird had been attacked and eaten by his cat. But the awe-inspiring magical power of controlling birds by whistling had already been deeply engraved into my mind.

The following years, wherever I went to places with trees and heard the sounds of birds, I had the habit of looking for nests. Unfortunately, I could never find a natural bird nest, not even once.

When I was about 15 years old, at one time going to my friend's house located on the campus of the University of Transport and Communications, I saw a bird nest falling down after a strong wind. It was the first time I saw a natural nest and could hold it in my own hands. The nest was made from dried Casuarina leaves, which had a golden-brown color. It was exquisitely made, truly beautiful! But there were no birds inside. Probably the nest was deserted after all the baby birds had already grown up into independent adults. It was fun but a little disappointing because I still could not find birds or eggs in that nest.

The desire to find a natural bird nest grew stronger as I grew older (and my career is generally not bird-related).

But my wish was granted when I was 40 years old. One time I brought my kids to our home in the countryside, Bắc Giang province, some 40 km north of Hanoi. On the way to the family graveyard surrounded by rice fields, I spotted something strange alongside a shrub. I approached to look closer and realized it was a big bird nest. The placement of the nest made it less likely to be noticed. Furthermore, located within the graveyard area with walls all around, it was not disturbed by local children. Looking inside, I was astonished to find five little bird eggs.

Two years later, I came across another bird's nest at the same graveyard. This one was inside the lush bushes of the *Bidens pilosa* daisies. The nest was absolutely beautiful, with just one egg inside (see Figure 3.3).

Figure 3.3: A flowerpecker nest in the graveyard, taken on March 26, 2013.

In 2015, for the first time, I finally knew how it felt like to see birds making a nest in my own garden, only several meters away from the house's wall. It was the nest of flowerpeckers, made from banana leaves together with trash they found around the place (quite similar to how the nest in Jardin Darcy was made). Thanks to observing the birds here, I did not miss the information about the trash bag on the tree in Darcy.

After all these long stories, I want to point out a very important thing in the serendipity mechanism of searching and quick information-assessing: the perceived values of the received information are based on accumulated information (existing knowledge), the evaluation of related information (where the relationship may not be recognized at the time), and information acquisition techniques. This background may be developed for a very long time. Time has two effects. On the one hand, waning values will be discarded. On the other hand, after multiple times of filtering, values that stay will cause even bigger questions (provoke stronger curiosity) when they emerge (be aware of). When pieces of information like the bird nest in Darcy or the birds drinking air conditioner's wastewater appear, they have such a strong impact to contribute to, inspire, and urge the completion of ongoing research projects. Whatever the case may be, the emergence of serendipity is due to how information is evaluated based on the integrated values within the current mindset of the person processing the information.

This is, in my opinion, the gateway into the mechanism of how serendipity arises.

3.3. The gateway to serendipity

What can be drawn from the stories above is that the process leading to serendipity needs conditions. Such conditions are the existent set of core values (or mindset) that shape how a person thinks and acts. A person can absorb various types of information in a moment, but when they enter the mind, they are assessed by the multi-filtering evaluation system. Only the information considered valuable (or beneficial) is allowed to get close to the mindset and influences subsequent thinking and behaviors. That system is simultaneously driven by both the information from the external environment and the core values. For instance, on the way to the MonoPrix supermarket, the chirps of baby birds were apparently not the only sound that I could hear at that moment, but also the vehicle sound on the street, the rustling sound of trees in the park, our walking sound on the pavement, etc. Since childhood, my special interest and curiosity about bird nests drew our attention to the baby birds' chirps and motivated us to find the nest the next morning.

While a person's current thinking about a subject is influenced by a set of previous information, knowledge, experiences, and feelings, it is worth asking an ontological question: "why do those knowledge, experiences, and feelings exist in my mind?" In other words, many things exist in this world, but why is my interest specifically in birds and bird nests compared to other species, like tiger, bear, or fish?

The mindsponge information-processing mechanism might answer this question. Each person has a distinct mindset and so forth distinct priorities, which can consciously or subconsciously direct the person's thinking and behaviors. Such priorities drive the appraisal process of absorbed information (either quick or strict) by subjectively giving value to that information based on related prior information, knowledge, experiences, and feelings. Therefore, two people can see different values when looking at the same thing. Deep in my mindset, I have had a very strong curiosity about the images of birds and bird nests since my childhood. If my curiosity about birds and bird nests were not significant enough so that it could become one of my priorities, I would not have been intrigued by information related to birds (e.g., the bird's nest in Darcy park, the scientific article about the bird on *Science*, the birds drinking contaminated water in Hanoi). However, if another person were me, they would have other priorities, so the thinking processes that I did would not occur, and nothing related to the semiconducting principle would not be proposed.

The mindset at the moment does not suddenly appear, but it is a product that is formulated, forged, and shaped through a continuous information processing process in the past. Given that storing information in the memory is energy consuming and a person's energy is limited, only information with the highest perceived value can be stored for a long time. Any information perceived as little beneficial was removed during the process for saving energy. The remaining information is used as references to evaluate the value of newly accepted information. During this process, information analogous to the remaining information will be favored and given more value than information that is not. Suppose there is no new information that can negate the remaining information. In that case, the value of the remaining information will be reinforced over time and eventually generate more influence on the person's thinking and behaviors.

A person's perceived value of a particular thing can be increased if their demand for that thing grows. In my case, the funny moment of my friend calling out loud and the eye-catching image of the bird's nest in the textbook are special catalysts that stimulate my curiosity about birds and bird nest information. Such curiosity drove me to question what natural birds and bird nests look like. Having questions in mind increased my perceived benefit of information involved with birds.

Consequently, it has my "radar" and information evaluation system that prioritizes noticing and absorbing birds' information.

Thus, it can be said that our cognitive growth begins from making questions. Having a question consciously or subconsciously generates demand for information in general and knowledge and wisdom, in particular, to answer that question. This demand increases the perceived benefits of information that can help satisfy our needs. Sometimes, striving to answer particular questions will lead us to make more questions, which helps expand our radars and evaluation system to more types of information. This, in my opinion, is the condition for cognitive progress, creativity, innovation, and serendipity. I am not sure if an animal can make a question by itself, but I know that most humans always make questions.

In terms of information processing and according to the mindsponge framework, when we decide to keep a piece of information in our memory when its values are still unknown or not yet carefully evaluated, such information is temporarily stored in the buffer zone. The buffer zone is a theoretical space within the mind where information is kept during the evaluating process or waiting to be evaluated. In the case of serendipity (regarding solving a specific problem), the seemingly "random" information is not discarded immediately after the initial scanning (quick evaluation) due to being accepted as a different value (not related to the specific problem being considered). However, in the new process, because its values concerning the unsolved problem are not yet established (as opposed to its accepted original value from the completed process), the information stays in the buffer zone awaiting further evaluation. The event of encountering the bird's nest in France had been waiting for some time in my mind before its values in relation to my research on the semiconducting environmental principle were clearly established (Vuong, 2021a).

In life, at any moment, there may be a lot of unanswered questions in one's mind demanding solutions. We need to keep a lot of unfinished evaluating processes simultaneously. Naturally, when many pieces of information are all competing for attention and a place in memory, the brain will prioritize those perceived to be more important. In my case, the bird's nest encounter has a special place in my mind stemming from my love for nature (and birds in particular), which caused the information to be accepted into my mindset mainly based on emotional values. In contrast, its values in relation to the mentioned environmental research still had not yet been well-evaluated. But other seemingly mundane events might not have such privilege to be kept when their values are still mostly unknown, and who knows if they could also be the keys to solving other important problems. They can be pushed back, left somewhere deep in the corner of my mind that becomes harder and harder to recall as time goes by. When new information keeps pouring in, some old ones may be forgotten, especially when we tend to perceive them as waning values before being able to realize them as precious missing pieces for some big problems in the future. We are often surprised when serendipity strikes, and maybe we would be even more surprised if we could ever know how many other potential strikes have been lost through the years.

A disciplined system of practices should be employed to support us in keeping potentially crucial information accurately. Such practices in scientific research contexts can include objectively recording data (external information sources) or quickly writing down interesting thoughts (internal information sources) (Vuong et al., 2022; Vuong &

Napier, 2014). Objective data recording can prevent unaware and biased information filtering in the person receiving information (Holman et al., 2015). It may also lead to skipping over small details that may prove important later. Immediately writing down interesting thoughts is helpful, especially when the ideas are still "young" and have not been sufficiently connected to other major theories or belief systems. Scientific preprint servers are convenient and effective platforms for these purposes (Q. H. Vuong, 2020). Building a disciplined operation is one of the three pillars in the 3D principle of innovative processes (Vuong & Napier, 2014).

The (seemingly subtle) conditionality of serendipity can be observed through some brilliant moments within the life of Pablo Picasso (1881-1973) – a worldwide famous artist, often known by the public for his extraordinary paintings in cubist and surreal styles. This Spanish artist went through many phases in his life, from poverty to huge success, with various layers of emotions toward major global events (such as World War I and II) as well as issues in his personal life. Picasso's paintings from 1901 to 1904 (known as his Blue Period) were mainly in blue shades, usually depicting a rather gloomy atmosphere. His style during this period was influenced by the suicide of one of his friends. Furthermore, there was also an urban legend about how Picasso might have gotten to this style when he ran out of paint except for the color blue and experimented with monochromatic paintings. During Picasso's African Period (1906-1909), his painting style was heavily influenced by African art, such as masks, sculptures, and ancient drawings. In 1907, upon viewing African art in a museum at the *Palais du Trocadéro*, Picasso had a moment of striking inspiration that later led to his famous painting *Les Demoiselles d'Avignon*, where the characters' faces were (partially) based on the Iberian sculptures and African totem art that he had collected or had been shown earlier. This period, particularly *Les Demoiselles d'Avignon,* served as the foundation for Picasso to develop and pioneer the revolutionizing style known as Cubism – one of the most influential art movements in the 20th century (Dasgupta, 2019).

Expressing his thoughts on the adventure of creating art, Picasso said, *"Je ne cherche pas, je trouve"* [I do not seek, I find]. While Picasso highly valued venturing into the uncertainty with confidence and comfort, we need to acknowledge two very important underlying conditions leading to this artist's outstanding achievements: his expertise in art and his mindset at each specific time before innovation. Firstly, it is clear that Picasso was very talented regarding painting. Even when only at the age of 14, he painted *Portrait of Aunt Pepa* – which art critic Juan Eduardo Cirlot praised as "without a doubt one of the greatest in the whole history of Spanish painting". This is essentially similar to the common advice of "getting ready for when the opportunity comes". In terms of information processing, a certain value can only be realized if the mind is currently capable of processing such value. This is the knowledge aspect of the conditional background. Secondly, Picasso had appropriate mental directions in relation to the "missing pieces" that made up the miraculous serendipity moments throughout his career. While many artists have witnessed the beauty of African art and the horror of war, Picasso was the one who connected all the right dots to produce *Les Demoiselles d'Avignon* and *Guernica* (Clark, 2013). In essence, Picasso asked the "right" questions, and thus he was open and prepared to receive the "missing pieces". In terms of information processing, a certain value is only perceived as useful if one needs such value. This is the navigational aspect of the conditional background. (We will discuss the conditionality in the mechanism of serendipity in further detail in Chapters 6 and 7.)

Similar patterns can also be seen in popular stories about some major scientific discoveries. We may all be familiar with the legend about Isaac Newton observing an apple falling (some said it fell right on his head), which made him ponder the phenomenon of an object falling and later led to his theory of gravity. Suppose the legend is generally correct, it is quite obvious that the observation of the falling apple cannot be the key to the theory if it was not for Newton's knowledge in physics and his existing big question about the nature of gravitation. Likewise, we can consider the famous legend about Archimedes' bathtub and his discovery of the method to measure the volume of an irregular-shaped object through water displacement. Without the knowledge and lingering questions in mind, the event might be just another mundane moment of watching bathwater spilling out. In brief, while the information (the phenomenon) stays objectively the same, its subjective value (in relation to one's problem required solving at that moment) is conditional and differs from person to person.

Chapter references

Clark, T. J. (2013). *Picasso and truth: from Cubism to Guernica* (Vol. 56). Princeton University Press.

Dasgupta, S. (2019). The complexity of creativity: Les Demoiselles D'Avignon as a cognitive-historical laboratory. *Creativity Research Journal, 31*(4), 377-394.

Holman, L., Head, M. L., Lanfear, R., & Jennions, M. D. (2015). Evidence of experimental bias in the life sciences: why we need blind data recording. *PLoS Biology, 13*(7), e1002190.

Napier, N., & Vuong, Q. H. (2013). Serendipity as a strategic advantage? In T. Wilkinson (Ed.), *Strategic management in the 21st century* (pp. 175-199). Praeger/ABC-Clio.

Nguyen, M.-H., & Vuong, Q.-H. (2021). Evaluation of the Aichi Biodiversity Targets: The international collaboration trilemma in interdisciplinary research. *Pacific Conservation Biology*. Online Early.

Nguyen, M.-H., Le, T.-T., Nguyen, H.-K. T., Ho, M.-T., Nguyen, H. T. T., & Vuong, Q.-H. (2021). Alice in Suicideland: Exploring the Suicidal Ideation Mechanism through the Sense of Connectedness and Help-Seeking Behaviors. *International Journal of Environmental Research and Public Health*, 18(7), 3681.

Thanh, V. (2021). *Vietnam PM calls for climate justice at COP26.* VNExpress International. Retrieved from (December 31, 2021) https://e.vnexpress.net/news/news/vietnam-pm-calls-for-climate-justice-at-cop26-4380258.html

Vuong, Q. H. (2016). Global mindset as the integration of emerging socio-cultural values through mindsponge processes: A transition economy perspective. In J. Kuada (Ed.), *Global mindsets: exploration and perspectives* (pp. 109-126). Routledge.

Vuong, Q. H. (2020). The rise of preprints and their value in social sciences and humanities. *Science Editing*, 7(1), 70-72.

Vuong, Q. H., & Napier, N. K. (2014). Making creativity: the value of multiple filters in the innovation process. *International Journal of Transitions and Innovation Systems*, 3(4), 294-327.

Vuong, Q. H., & Napier, N. K. (2015). Acculturation and global mindsponge: An emerging market perspective. *International Journal of Intercultural Relations*, 49, 354-367.

Vuong, Q.-H. (2020). From children's literature to sustainability science, and young scientists for a more sustainable Earth. *Journal of Sustainability Education*, 24(3), 1-12. http://www.susted.com/wordpress/content/from-childrens-literature-to-sustainability-science-and-young-scientists-for-a-more-sustainable-earth_2020_12/

Vuong, Q.-H. (2021a). The semiconducting principle of monetary and environmental values exchange. *Economics and Business Letters, 10*(3), 284-290.

Vuong, Q.-H. (2021b). Western monopoly of climate science is creating an eco-deficit culture. *Economy, Land & Climate Insight.* https://elc-insight.org/western-monopoly-of-climate-science-is-creating-an-eco-deficit-culture/

Vuong, Q.-H., Le, T.-T., La, V.-P., Nguyen, T. T. H., Ho, M.-T., Khuc, Q., & Nguyen, M.-H. (2022). Covid-19 vaccines production and societal immunization under the serendipity-mindsponge-3D knowledge management theory and conceptual framework. *Humanities and Social Sciences Communications, 9,* 22.

Kingfisher

©2017 Bui Quang Khiem

Chapter 4:
Serendipity as a survival skill

Quan-Hoang Vuong

This chapter is dedicated to the hypothesis that serendipity is a survival skill. The motive behind serendipity is one's desire to survive, and its outcomes increase one's survivability. Humans are always under existential threats due to stress from the natural or social environment, so serendipity – the ability to notice valuable information in relation to one's problem-solving processes – is crucial in terms of human survival. We can see this property in innovations on various levels, from minor and individual to major and collective.

4.1. Personal story

Mã đề (in Vietnamese) is a popular medicinal plant in Vietnam, called 车前草 (chē qián cǎo) in Chinese. *Mã đề* has the scientific name *Plantago asiatica* (Chinese plantain) – sometimes called *Mã đề á* – but local people also refer to the closely related species *Plantago major* (broadleaf plantain). The medicinal properties of *Mã đề* were well studied by Professor Đỗ Tất Lợi (Đỗ, 2015). Many Vietnamese families are quite familiar with this plant - which is often used to heal hot flashes or urinary tract inflammation. Of course, I do not always think of *mã đề*, but there were three times serendipity moments related to the plant have saved me.

https://doi.org/10.2478/9788366675865-010

The first time was in 2018. My family traveled from Dijon (France) to Geneva (Switzerland). We stayed on the bus for a long time and then walked in hot weather without drinking much water. My big toe joint became painfully swollen. But visiting a doctor there would be difficult to plan. Back in Dijon, when I was walking across Darcy Park, I found something similar to the *mã đề*, but with smoother and thinner leaves. I guessed it was the plant but could not confirm nor find reference materials, so I had to try it.

Figure 4.1: *Plantago* in a forest near Grenoble, France, taken on July 1, 2019. (The author with the blue hat examining a plant.)

I picked up some to check thoroughly. The shape of the leaf and its vein matched that of *mã đề*. Additionally, the plant's distinct flower can also be used for identification. At the time, it was not their blooming season, but I found one plant with a small flower bud. It was indeed the *mã đê*. So, I picked a couple of dozens back to make medicine for my swollen foot. I carefully cleaned them with water (who knows what the dogs might do in the park). Then I put them into boiled water and drank when it became cool enough. Merely three days later, the pain, as well as the swelling, decreased noticeably. My foot was healed completely after five or six days. Figure 4.1 shows I was collecting Plantago asiatica in 2019 in a forest near Grenoble, France.

The second time was when my wife had tooth pain when we were in Prague (Czech Republic). In general, going to the dentist would be very inconvenient in many ways. Luckily, when visiting Karlštejn Castle (about 30km from Prague), I found some *mã đê* plants. I picked some from the castle, and my wife's tooth problem was solved smoothly. I also shared what I knew about the plants with my friend from Bratislava, who joined our trip.

Lately, in December 2021, my leg hurt from playing sports and the cold weather. And once again, the *Mã đê* plants came to help. This time, the injury was probably a bit more serious, and recovery was slow.

Some ancient legends about the origin of *mã đê* are also typical stories of serendipity. While these legends differ in details about specific eras and characters, the main content is basically the same. In ancient China, due to the hot and dry weather, many soldiers had urinary problems that caused fatigue. However, someone noticed that the horses that ate a certain plant did not have such urinary problems. This observation led to the discovery of the diuretic property of *mã đê*. The plants were boiled with water to create a medicine that greatly helped the soldiers in those stories. Since the plant was found in front of horse wagons, people named it 车前草 (the grass before the horse wagon). Additionally, the Vietnamese name *mã đê* (literally: horse hoof) might have originated from the fact that these plants are often found in places near horses' footprints. Interestingly, how I came up with the connection between this story and the discussion on serendipity mechanism in this book is itself also the result of a serendipity strike involving my memories about *mã đề* being put through the mindsponge filtering processes in my mind.

The information absorption mechanism, as I remember, was initiated a long time ago. That was in a very different situation. At that time, my daughter was around five years old. One day in the summer, I caught a couple of cicadas that had not molted. I brought them home and gave them to my daughter.

When I was young, that time was around 1977-1980, one of the popular summer games was cicada and cricket collecting [bắt ve và đổ dế]. It was because of the noisy sound produced by the cicada. The sound is like a call prompting the kids to pour onto the street. At about 5:30 every afternoon, the cicada started calling. At that time, toys were rare, so gathering and collecting cicadas with friends was a way to have fun. Until later, I recognized that cicada collecting was simply catching a cicada, putting it in a pocket, and waiting to see it molt into the adult stage. It was nothing special. But, what gave it meaningful values is the social matters. Gathering, tempting to catch cicada, chatting, and showing off the number or the uniqueness of caught cicadas were social activities. When participating in these activities, the kids could feel that they belonged to the collective. The social meanings of cicada collecting could be manifested in the case of a kid abandoned by the social group for some reason. He still searched and collected cicada, but there was no more amusement. When he found a cicada, I also witnessed that he did not catch it but tried to call the group and let them catch it. This is an effort to reintegrate into the social group through a cicada. After all, the cicadas' values were the amusement perceived when being in a small-scale society formed by several kids. That society had its own culture, rules, and standards, of which the cicada represented the value system. If the cicada collecting game is played for a sufficient amount of time, the image of cicadas will become a representative cultural value.

Back to my daughter when I brought the cicada home. She looked at the cicada with no affection at all and was even frightened. She remained wary of the insect and tried to study this strange creature. It was completely opposite to my imagination that she would become enthusiastic after receiving the cicada. Then I realized that I was unreasonable because the cicada did not hold any value or belief for my daughter. She had never seen the social role of a cicada in connecting people or felt sad because the cicada flew away right when she could almost catch it.

Precisely speaking, participation in cicada collecting manifests the right of being a member of the small-scale society of kids during summertime. Being left out of the activity, to some extent, is equivalent to not being existent. The feeling of non-existence is a terrifying experience. Although it cannot be put into words, any kid is afraid of experiencing such feelings. By striving to collect and gain more "medals" (or cicadas) than others, a kid could show the ability of a "professional". When a kid continuously acquired high performance, they could improve their rank within the group; in other words, they were considered to belong to a higher class. Respect for the kid was almost "default" if they were in a higher class. The techniques of catching cicada were indifferent, so the ability to detect cicada through inquiring about the probability of cicadas' occurrences was more important than skills (e.g., climbing, groping). Based on these observations, I proposed a new hypothesis of serendipity: Serendipity is one of the fundamental abilities of humans that appear early during one's lifetime and has a direct association with humans' survival methods.

4.2. Proposed hypothesis

Arguably the basic mission of humanity as a species is to survive and extend human existence to future generations; naturally, this leads to desires to become the "fittest" in one's environment and overcome existential threats, as suggested by the Darwinist theory of evolution (Darwin, 2003). The struggles for survival are not only limited to finding food, shelter, or avoiding predators that we often see in ancient human society. Existential threats are always present, and desires for surviving never cease. In chapter 5, we will take a closer look at examples of how serendipity led to human ancestors' major innovations as well as survival motives in social contexts. Now, let us first look at some familiar examples.

Modern antibiotics are almost taken for granted in today's world, and many people may forget that they all started from the invention of penicillin just in the last century. In 1928, Alexander Fleming observed some Petri dishes containing *Staphylococcus* bacteria and noticed something strange in one dish. The *Staphylococcus* colonies did not appear in the area where a type of mold was growing (later identified as *Penicillium notatum*). This serendipity moment was what led to the large-scale production of penicillin as an antibiotic for human treatment during World War II. Without antibiotics, infections, even from small injuries, can become life-threatening problems. Notably, in the 1918 influenza pandemic that killed more than 50 million people, most deaths were attributed to secondary bacterial pneumonia (Sheng et al., 2011). While the issue of secondary bacterial pneumonia is also present in the ongoing Covid-19 pandemic, the widespread use of antibiotics today greatly reduces the severity of the disease. It contributes to the lower mortality rate compared to the 1918 pandemic (Ginsburg & Klugman, 2020).

Another important point about the Covid-19 pandemic was that the miraculously rapid vaccine development was not due to pure luck or being carelessly rushed. Still, it was systematically based on our collective knowledge, including the use of prior sequencing of the human genome and SARS-CoV-2 genome (Kames et al., 2020), as well as decades of vaccine research. The Covid-19 vaccine development, production, and distribution process can be considered an information process that includes the application of serendipity together with the mindsponge information filtering framework and the 3D principles of creativity (Napier & Vuong, 2013; Vuong et al., 2022; Vuong & Napier, 2014). Additionally, there have been other adaptive changes in our social systems as well (Huynh, 2020; Pham & Ho, 2020). The drive from survival desires helps set the conditions for serendipity through making preparations in terms of knowledge as well as the "big questions". To find the "missing pieces", survival purposes determine the "what" while the mindsponge mechanism (Nguyen et al., 2021; Vuong, 2016; Vuong & Napier, 2015) and the 3D principles determine the "how" (Vuong & Napier, 2014).

When thinking about a "golden age" of impactful innovations across recent global history, we often refer to the glorified Industrial Revolution in the 18th and 19th centuries, started by breakthroughs in manufacturing processes and systems in Great Britain (Chiến & Hoàng, 2015). But were these powerful initiatives mainly driven by humanity's noble pursuits of intellect and virtue?

Professor Priya Satia, an expert of modern British history from Standford University, argued that the Industrial Revolution in Britain began with the need for war supplies (Satia, 2019). "We need to stop thinking that Britain invented industrialism because it had an especially laissez-faire government or because it had a unique entrepreneurial genius or culture," Professor Priya Satia said. "Let's acknowledge the fact that Britain was involved in a lot of wars, and in order to pursue those wars, the government needed arms. And the British government clearly encouraged innovation within their gun industry." (Satia, 2018).

Human history is filled with conflicts, big and small, direct and subtle. Breakthroughs fueled by desires to overpower one's enemies were not limited to military innovations but also the development of social systems; from early politics and institutions to modern weapons and advanced warfare and governance, innovation holds the central position in humans' long and rather gruesome history of war (Lee, 2016). While intraspecific conflicts exist in many animals, humans are special for our ability to formulate complex strategies and find ways to manipulate opposing groups (Von Clausewitz, 2008). As the famous ancient book "The Art of War" suggests, a good strategy and its execution require not only military prowess as background conditions but also the ability to notice and assess information from direct observation on the battlefields (Tzu, 2021). Humans always aim to survive and thrive to ensure even better survival chances in the future. The desire to become the "fittest" in both natural and social environments motivates people to seek information that helps achieve such goals. This is the base for innovations - the power for gaining an edge in the never-ending survival battle.

Considering the significance of serendipity in innovation, we propose that serendipity – the ability to notice useful information in one's surroundings – is a survival skill. As discussed in the preceding chapters, the ability to notice useful information is a conditional process leading to the observable results (deemed unexpected) of serendipity moments. Persons or groups that can make the best use of serendipity will gain advantages in terms of survival – in both natural contexts (biological mortality) and social contexts ("success" in various human aspects).

Chapter references

Chiến, B. N., & Hoàng, V. Q. (2015). *Bằng chứng cuộc sống: Suy ngẫm về phát triển bền vững Việt Nam*. Nhà xuất bản Chính trị Quốc gia Sự Thật.

Darwin, C. (2003). *On the origin of species* (D. Knight, Ed. Reprint ed.). Routledge.

Đỗ, T. L. (2015). *Những cây thuốc và vị thuốc Việt Nam* (19 ed.). NXB Hồng Đức.

Ginsburg, A. S., & Klugman, K. P. (2020). COVID-19 pneumonia and the appropriate use of antibiotics. *The Lancet Global Health*, *8*(12), e1453-e1454.

Huynh, T. L. D. (2020). Does culture matter social distancing under the COVID-19 pandemic? *Safety Science, 130*, 104872.

Kames, J., Holcomb, D. D., Kimchi, O., DiCuccio, M., Hamasaki-Katagiri, N., Wang, T., ... Kimchi-Sarfaty, C. (2020). Sequence analysis of SARS-CoV-2 genome reveals features important for vaccine design. *Scientific Reports, 10*(1), 15643.

Lee, W. E. (2016). *Waging war: conflict, culture, and innovation in world history*. Oxford University Press.

Napier, N., & Vuong, Q. H. (2013). Serendipity as a strategic advantage? In T. Wilkinson (Ed.), *Strategic management in the 21st century* (pp. 175-199). Praeger/ABC-Clio.

Nguyen, M.-H., Le, T.-T., Nguyen, H.-K. T., Ho, M.-T., Nguyen, H. T. T., & Vuong, Q.-H. (2021). Alice in Suicideland: Exploring the Suicidal Ideation Mechanism through the Sense of Connectedness and Help-Seeking Behaviors. *International Journal of Environmental Research and Public Health, 18*(7), 3681.

Pham, H.-H., & Ho, T.-T.-H. (2020). Toward a 'new normal' with e-learning in Vietnamese higher education during the post-COVID-19 pandemic. *Higher Education Research & Development, 39*(7), 1327–1331.

Satia, P. (2018). *War drove 18th-century Industrial Revolution in Great Britain*. Stanford News. Retrieved from (December 25, 2021) https://news.stanford.edu/2018/05/03/war-drove-18th-century-industrial-revolution-great-britain/

Satia, P. (2019). *Empire of guns: the violent making of the Industrial Revolution*. Stanford University Press.

Sheng, Z. M., Chertow, D. S., Ambroggio, X., McCall, S., Przygodzki, R. M., Cunningham, R. E., ... Taubenberger, J. K. (2011). Autopsy series of 68 cases dying before and during the 1918 influenza pandemic peak. *Proceedings of the National Academy of Sciences, 108*(39), 16416-16421.

Tzu, S. (2021). *The art of war*. Vintage.

Von Clausewitz, C. (2008). *On war*. Princeton University Press.

Vuong, Q. H. (2016). Global mindset as the integration of emerging socio-cultural values through mindsponge processes: A transition economy perspective. In J. Kuada (Ed.), *Global mindsets: exploration and perspectives* (pp. 109-126). Routledge.

Vuong, Q. H., & Napier, N. K. (2014). Making creativity: the value of multiple filters in the innovation process. *International Journal of Transitions and Innovation Systems, 3*(4), 294-327.

Vuong, Q. H., & Napier, N. K. (2015). Acculturation and global mindsponge: An emerging market perspective. *International Journal of Intercultural Relations, 49,* 354-367.

Vuong, Q.-H., Le, T.-T., La, V.-P., Nguyen, T. T. H., Ho, M.-T., Khuc, Q., & Nguyen, M.-H. (2022). Covid-19 vaccines production and societal immunization under the serendipity-mindsponge-3D knowledge management theory and conceptual framework. *Humanities and Social Sciences Communications, 9,* 22.

Kingfisher

©2017 Bui Quang Khiem

Chapter 5:
Natural and social survival: the drivers of serendipity

Tam-Tri Le

Survival motives for serendipity can be categorized into two types: natural and social. Natural survival motives refer to the desire to prolong one's physical existence. On a collective level, this is the existence of the human species. Social survival motives refer to the desire to gain social power (competitive advantage) as well as to prolong the existence of mental and social constructs (such as identity, ideologies, etc.). Similarly, social survival motives can be applied on an individual or collective level.

5.1. Problem solving and demand for information

As we know it on this planet, life has a natural tendency: to survive – in other words, to prolong its existence as much as possible. In this sense, reproduction is survival on the collective scale. Why does life have such a desire to sustain its existence? This is a trillion-dollar question in biology and philosophy. Regardless, humans also follow the tendency of trying to survive. The concept of "survival" in human contexts can sometimes be as simple and straightforward as in all other creatures. It can also be much more complex on various social aspects and levels (see further discussions in later sections in this chapter). Whichever the case may be, the base of the general thinking process

https://doi.org/10.2478/9788366675865-011

for human behaviors driven by survival motives might follow simple logic. First, we have a need for something (desires), then we think about how to achieve it (asking questions). The act of asking questions can be deemed a way to demand useful information to achieve the goals that fulfill the corresponding desires.

We do not fully know if animals formulate questions in their heads or not, but we can be sure that humans constantly ask questions. Regarding desires in humans, we can look at the well-known Maslow's hierarchy of needs (Maslow, 1943). Our needs are not automatically fulfilled upon desiring it. After asking the question of how to achieve the desired target, we will intentionally search for information. In brief, this is a problem-solving process. The harder the problems, the harder it is to find useful information that leads to solutions. For example, when the purpose of surviving is weakened, as, in the case of suicidality, the value of self-killing might negate other values of behaviors involving life prolongation (Nguyen et al., 2021; Vuong et al., 2021). When survival desires (including desires to outcompete in environments with limited resources) are the goal in the questions, those who are better at getting useful information will have advantages over others. Whether it is the matter of biological mortality or social competition, serendipity – to be precise, the ability to notice valuable information in the environment – can be considered a survival "skill" that helps individuals or the whole population gain an edge in the relentless battle of life (Vuong et al., 2022). The following sections in this chapter will provide evidence for the book's hypothesis in natural and social survival contexts: serendipity is one of the fundamental abilities of humans that appear early during one's lifetime and is directly associated with human survival methods.

5.2. Natural survival

All biological organisms on Earth have two main instinctual missions: survival and reproduction. Here we consider both the survival of individuals and their respective species. Existential threats go side by side with the natural desire to prolong one's existence. More than 99% of all species ever lived have gone extinct since the beginning of life (biological organisms) on this planet. Over the course of 3.5 billion years, life has emerged, destroyed, and evolved. In the last half a billion years, the ecosphere has gone through five mass extinction events as well as many "minor" ones. Coming to existence after the fifth mass extinction, humans wonder if the next mass extinction would occur any time soon. Unfortunately, as argued by Elizabeth Kolbert in her book "The Sixth Extinction: An Unnatural History", we are already in the sixth mass extinction – one heavily influenced by the human factor (Kolbert, 2014). For example, think of the severely disruptive impacts of the Covid-19 pandemic (Schell et al., 2020).

Available evidence of the earliest human ancestors was probably *Homo habilis* ("handy man") found in Africa, dating back more than two million years ago. Next in the timeline was *Homo erectus* ("upright man"), appearing before the emergence of our species – *Homo sapiens* ("modern man"), about 300 thousand years ago. However, at the moment, we still do not have sufficient evidence to precisely trace many aspects involving the origin of modern human ancestors (Bergström et al., 2021). Compared to humans, some other species have survived a very long time. For example, modern crocodiles are almost identical to how they were about 200 thousand years ago, while sharks might have survived for about 400 thousand years. Cyanobacteria are probably the oldest organisms in terms of total survival time – 3.5 billion years; they have been living on this planet since the earliest era of the ecosphere. Having the highest intellectual capacity among all living species on the planet, humans are actually having difficulties extending our existence to a small fraction of these "old" species. We are proud that the human brain is the pinnacle of biological evolution, but is our species really the fittest in terms of survival?

In 1859, Charles Darwin originally published the book "*On the Origin of Species*", which is now well-known as the foundation for the modern science of evolution (Darwin, 2003). The notion of "natural selection" was later suggested to refer to "survival of the fittest", which was coined by Herbert Spencer several years before Darwin's publication in 1859 (Spencer, 2020). Biological survival is prioritized over other types of desire (e.g., emotional or intellectual) regarding motives behind behaviors when we consider Maslow's hierarchy of needs – the first two levels being physiological and safety needs, respectively (Maslow, 1943).

In humans, adaptation has been far beyond genetics and physiology since we established social systems to "inherit" priorly developed knowledge and tools. Archaeologists and anthropologists found evidence suggesting that the formation and evolution of human society were strategically driven by both individual and collective (species-wide) purposes of survival and reproduction in the fierce battle of living in nature (Watson, 2007). In this sense, a useful innovation can be analogous to growing a new limb that is competitively advantageous. Thus, serendipity – noticing valuable information from one's environment – might act as the base for inventions that give individuals, groups, and the entire human race a better chance in the battle of survival.

Without the ability to recognize valuable information from observing countless phenomena constantly happening in the environment, humans would not have been able to make the crucial early breakthroughs that we often take for granted today, such as fire, cooking, tools, and agriculture. The most well-aware important invention in the early history of humanity was to make and control fire, which was a major factor that drove human evolution (Gowlett, 2016). The big questions here should have been "how to sustain natural fire?" and then "how to create fire?" Based on these directions, humans started to collect related information.

Human ancestors could not just know how to make fire out of the blue; rather, they might first observe and evaluate the values of natural fires (e.g., being a light source, scaring animals, making foods tasty and easily digestible). Over a very long course of several hundred thousand years, these perceived values led to more sophisticated methods of creating and maintaining fires. The observation of natural fires can be considered a serendipity moment (or a "missing piece") when we take into account the whole lengthy process until controlling fire became an integrated part of human society. During this process, the values of fire needed to be stored (within the collective knowledge system) and continuously be evaluated concerning the everlasting primal question of how to increase our chance of survival; otherwise, just like in other animals, the values will be lost after the immediate generation.

Regarding the big questions on food for early humans, they should have been "what are edible?", "what are more nutritious?" and "what can be mass-produced?", in that order. Studies on the origin of agriculture revealed that ancient humans had a very long history of establishing their grain-based diets (Choi, 2016). About 2.5 million years ago (Lower Paleolithic), humans gathered random plants. About 300 thousand years ago (Middle Paleolithic), humans started to focus on more nutritious plants; and the use of edible plants became more sophisticated about 50 thousand years ago (Upper Paleolithic). Various types of grass seeds intentionally collected from wild grasses were the staple foods of the Chinese about 30 thousand years ago (Wang et al., 2016). The transition from foraging to grain agriculture shared similarities between cultivating rice and millet in China and wheat and barley in West Asia. Wild grass seeds were found to be used as staple foods in the Israel region 23 thousand years ago (Weiss et al., 2004). In this early time, humans needed to be able to notice edible and nutritious items among a lot of random objects they encountered in the wild. The ability to notice valuable information from the natural environment was a matter of life and death when sufficient food supply was a major daily concern.

While survival motives in terms of sustenance are not always so raw and direct – especially in the modern era, the skills for recognizing valuable information from one's surroundings have led to delightful discoveries in food and cuisine throughout human history. Some popular foods we are familiar with today are the results of interesting serendipity moments in the past. For example, humans started to consume cheese more than 4000 years ago, together with the story of an Arabian merchant who accidentally made cheese while going across a desert as he stored milk inside a sheep's stomach (containing rennet) and discovered the delicious curd after a while in the hot weather (International Dairy Foods Association, 2021). Quite similarly, yogurt – a fermented milk product used in many different regions across the globe since thousands of years ago – was discovered by herdsmen who kept milk in bags made from animal intestines (Fisberg & Machado, 2015). Other fermented products such as beer and pickles are also often believed to have been accidentally discovered.

Regarding the origin of modern-day coffee use, there was a story about a goat herder in Ethiopia who observed that goats eating the berries of a certain tree became energetic and could not sleep; he later shared his findings with the local monastery and made a drink from those berries, which later led to the start of coffee cultivation on the Arabian Peninsula in the 15th century (National Coffee Association USA, 2021). Some ancient legends also suggest that tofu was made accidentally in China during the Han dynasty before becoming a popular food across many East and Southeast Asian countries. In recent times, by chance, we have also created several popular modern foods such as popsicles, potato chips, corn flakes, and chocolate chip cookies.

The human species is heavily reliant on tool use. Even our ancestors started to develop an organized production of stone tools about 2.6 million years ago – known as Oldowan tools (Braun et al., 2019), which made human ancestors significantly stand out from other primates. Some familiar animals such as monkeys, crows, sea otters, and octopuses can intentionally use objects they found in their surroundings to help achieve certain goals. Our genetically close relatives – the chimpanzees – can use twigs to "fish" termites for a tasty snack. However, while other animals may figure out the values of objects (or observed phenomena, etc.) temporarily and individually, humans, with effective social communication, try to make connections to "bigger questions" and incorporate such values into an inheritable collective knowledge system (can be seen as culture). This again reflects serendipity's nature of conditionality. Standing on an established culture, humans can turn "one-time interesting things" into breakthroughs for the long-term advancement of the collective system. Regarding the concept of serendipity presented in this book, this point helps demonstrate a piece of information being a "missing piece" of an intentional and systemic investigation in contrast to being a lucky coincidence with disconnected values.

5.3. Social survival

Within populations of many animals, those with more adaptive genetics (in the current living environment) normally have more advantages in reproduction so that the next generations may have higher survival chances. Herbert Spencer applied the principles of natural evolution to human society, forming the theory of "social Darwinism". This expresses the idea that competitions within human society are a form of "survival of the fittest," which drives the improvement (social evolution) of the collective. While this view can be used to create the foundation for deeper conceptual development on the underlying drive of social progress, we should be careful when basing arguments on former interpretations such as from the works of Thomas Malthus or Herbert Spencer (Rogers, 1972). As value perception in humans can be very individually specific and context-based, making induction from complex social phenomena will need an integral approach.

In humans, regarding both individual and collective perspectives, survival (and reproduction) is not simply the matter of biological mortality. Still, we also desire to sustain (and expand) the existence of various mental and social constructs such as identities, ideologies, or personal possessions. In a sense, it can be thought of the natural self-preservation tendencies in social contexts, knowledge or financial growth, or even the desire to leave behind a glorious legacy after one's biological death. Likewise, competitions for resources or better living conditions can be beyond biological drives like other animals (e.g., increasing mating chances or taking better care of offspring), although they may share similar patterns. In Maslow's hierarchy of needs, we can see that, beyond the two base levels of physiological and safety needs, humans also desire love/belongingness, esteem, and self-actualization (Maslow, 1943). The former two levels are more driven by "natural survival" while the latter three are more driven by "social survival".

Human society has now been facing existential threats from environmental destruction and internal conflicts (Diamond, 2011). The global population is on the rise and will probably become around 10 billion people in the next several decades (Adam, 2021). The near future of the Earth's natural environment is a focus of concern, with the elephant in the room being climate change (United Nations, 2021). And while the collective still has not shown sufficient mindset changes in relation to nature (Vuong, 2021), we should brace for impact since disasters are already coming (Harvey, 2021; Tollefson, 2021). Long story short, humans are under environmental and social stress, as our species has always been. Fueled by the desire to become stronger and more well-adapted in society, in social contexts, we also rely on serendipity – specifically, the survival skill of noticing valuable information.

Many urban people around the world are quite familiar with Starbucks – a famous brand of multinational coffeehouse chain. In 2021, the corporate had net revenue of nearly 25 billion USD. But back in the 1970s and early 1980s, Starbucks was only a medium-size company selling coffee beans and brewing machines in the local area of Seattle, Washington. In 1983, Howard Schultz – working as Starbucks's Director of Retail Operations and Marketing at the time – was sent to Milan to attend a conference. While in Italy, Schultz took a detour from the conference and visited local cafés to see the European culture of coffee consumption. Upon observing the locals, Schultz realized that many Italian people did not come to cafés just for the sake of drinking coffee but rather to spend time together and talk with other customers. This serendipity moment gave Schultz the idea that instead of simply selling coffee, Starbucks should focus more on the café's settings, serving as a place for communal activities and interactions – in other words, a social hub. The direction change later led to the exponential growth of Starbucks chains in the US and global expansion. Howard Schultz held the position of Starbucks's chief executive officer (CEO) from 1986 to 2000 and again from 2008 to 2017. As of December 2021, Schultz is a billionaire with an estimated net worth of about 5 billion USD (Forbes, 2021).

Howard Schultz's ability to notice the value of the information about Milan's local coffee culture concerning the company's business helped him achieve great success in his career, improving his wealth and the status of his identity. It is also worth noting that in Schultz's early life, his family was relatively poor, meaning there should have been a high degree of "survival" stress. The desire to become successful in his career was a strong motive. In other words, the big question of how to achieve that purpose was in the back of his mind, thus serving as the navigation and condition for the directional connection of values when the "missing piece" was recognized – a serendipity moment. Regarding the aspect of social competitions (comparing with other fellow humans), Schultz's skills for catching that particular serendipity moment in the early 1980s (when others did not) paid off wonderfully. It gave him massive advantages in terms of social survival (e.g., financial gain, security, control, and influence). Additionally, Schultz will surely leave behind a noticeable legacy (prolonging the existence of his representative values) even when he is gone.

The significance of the social survival aspect can also be seen on collective levels. The status of the Starbucks company in the early 1980s was the background condition for Schultz's discovery. A strong desire for growth was a shared value within the company's collective mindset at the time, which, likewise, expressed as the lingering question "how". Suppose that the company has had no desires for growth and competition at all, they would not have welcomed the sudden innovative idea from Schultz. Regarding the impact of the innovation, it is obvious how much Starbucks has outcompeted other companies in the business. The existence of their brand in society has been greatly reinforced, and the chain has been expanded widely all over the globe. Naturally, all businesses today highly value serendipity for the competitive advantage it brings (Napier & Vuong, 2013; Vuong & Napier, 2014).

We do not even need to look at examples of huge successes to realize the social survival aspect of serendipity. Such miraculous moments can happen in everyone's daily life in human society, regardless of how personal or mundane their values appear in the eyes of others. Take intimate relationships for consideration; they are undoubtedly a major part of a normal human life. For most people in modern society, the initial encounter with one's intimate partner may be deemed a "lucky miracle" upon looking back. Finding the right partner can be considered serendipity driven by social survival motives: it usually starts from unexpected "discoveries" of each other; it increases social influence toward each other; it brings happiness, fulfilling certain personal and emotional needs; it may lead to the formation of a family (the usual preparation for having and raising children – extending one's social influence through ensuring the existence and well-being of future generations).

Almost all humans desire social success in one way or another (including all meanings one may give to the concept of success). Our information-seeking behaviors are based on the underlying aim to achieve such goals (Vuong & Napier, 2015; Vuong, 2016). We can all reflect on our own memory and find some moments in our lives when suddenly noticing certain useful pieces of information resulted in advantages for our social life in various degrees. In terms of social power, the impacts can be something "small" (e.g., having a nice conversation, making a good impression in front of friends) to something "big" personally (e.g., finding a dream job, meeting one's future spouse), or more rarely, even something "great" (e.g., discovering a million-dollar solution, starting a global trend). Those with better skills to notice more useful information in relation to their high-value demands ("big questions") will likely gain greater sustainability for their mental and social constructs.

Chapter references

Adam, D. (2021). How far will global population rise? Researchers can't agree. *Nature, 597*, 462-465.

Bergström, A., Stringer, C., Hajdinjak, M., Scerri, E. M. L., & Skoglund, P. (2021). Origins of modern human ancestry. *Nature, 590*, 229-237.

Braun, D. R., Aldeias, V., Archer, W., Arrowsmith, J. R., Baraki, N., Campisano, C. J., ... Reed, K. E. (2019). Earliest known Oldowan artifacts at >2.58 Ma from Ledi-Geraru, Ethiopia, highlight early technological diversity. *Proceedings of the National Academy of Sciences, 116*(24), 11712-11717.

Choi, C. (2016). Ancient Chinese may have cultivated grass seeds 30,000 years ago. *PNAS Journal Club.*

https://blog.pnas.org/2016/03/journal-club-ancient-chinese-may-have-cultivated-grass-seeds-30000-years-ago/

Darwin, C. (2003). *On the origin of species* (D. Knight, Ed. Reprint ed.). Routledge.

Diamond, J. M. (2011). *Collapse: how societies choose to fail or survive*. Penguin Books.

Fisberg, M., & Machado, R. (2015). History of yogurt and current patterns of consumption. *Nutrition Reviews*, *73*(S1), 4-7.

Forbes. (2021). *Howard Schultz*. Forbes. Retrieved from (January 11, 2022) https://www.forbes.com/profile/howard-schultz/

Gowlett, J. A. J. (2016). The discovery of fire by humans: a long and convoluted process. *Philosophical Transactions of the Royal Society B: Biological Sciences*, *371*(1696).

Harvey, F. (2021). *Climate experts warn world leaders 1.5C is 'real science', not just talking point*. The Guardian. Retrieved from (January 11, 2022) https://www.theguardian.com/environment/2021/oct/30/climate-experts-warn-world-leaders-15c-is-real-science-not-just-talking-point

International Dairy Foods Association. (2021). *History of cheese*. International Dairy Foods Association. Retrieved from (January 15, 2022) https://www.idfa.org/news-views/media-kits/cheese/history-of-cheese

Kolbert, E. (2014). *The sixth extinction: an unnatural history* (First Edition). Henry Holt and Company.

Maslow, A. H. (1943). A theory of human motivation. *Psychological Review*, *50*(4), 370-396.

Napier, N., & Vuong, Q. H. (2013). Serendipity as a strategic advantage? In T. Wilkinson (Ed.), *Strategic management in the 21st century* (pp. 175-199). Praeger/ABC-Clio.

National Coffee Association USA. (2021). *The history of coffee*. National Coffee Association USA. Retrieved from (December 26, 2021) https://www.ncausa.org/about-coffee/history-of-coffee

Nguyen, M.-H., Le, T.-T., Nguyen, H.-K. T., Ho, M.-T., Nguyen, H. T. T., & Vuong, Q.-H. (2021). Alice in Suicideland: exploring the suicidal ideation mechanism through the sense of connectedness and help-seeking behaviors. *International Journal of Environmental Research and Public Health, 18*(7), 3681.

Rogers, J. A. (1972). Darwinism and Social Darwinism. *Journal of the History of Ideas, 33*(2), 265.

Schell, D., Wang, M., & Huynh, T. L. D. (2020). This time is indeed different: A study on global market reactions to public health crisis. *Journal of Behavioral and Experimental Finance, 27*, 100349.

Spencer, H. (2020). *The principles of biology: Volume 1*. Outlook Verlag.

Tollefson, J. (2021). Top climate scientists are sceptical that nations will rein in global warming. *Nature, 599*, 22-24.

United Nations. (2021). *Secretary-General calls latest IPCC Climate Report 'code red for humanity', stressing 'irrefutable' evidence of human influence*. United Nations Meetings Coverage and Press Releases. Retrieved from (December 26, 2021) https://www.un.org/press/en/2021/sgsm20847.doc.htm

Vuong, Q. H. (2016). Global mindset as the integration of emerging socio-cultural values through mindsponge processes: A transition economy perspective. In J. Kuada (Ed.), *Global mindsets: exploration and perspectives* (pp. 109-126). Routledge.

Vuong, Q. H., & Napier, N. K. (2014). Making creativity: the value of multiple filters in the innovation process. *International Journal of Transitions and Innovation Systems, 3*(4), 294-327.

Vuong, Q.-H. (2021). The semiconducting principle of monetary and environmental values exchange. *Economics and Business Letters, 10*(3), 284-290.

Vuong, Q.-H., & Napier, N. K. (2015). Acculturation and global mindsponge: an emerging market perspective. *International Journal of Intercultural Relations, 49,* 354-367.

Vuong, Q.-H., Le, T.-T., La, V.-P., Nguyen, T. T. H., Ho, M.-T., Khuc, Q., & Nguyen, M.-H. (2022). Covid-19 vaccines production and societal immunization under the serendipity-mindsponge-3D knowledge management theory and conceptual framework. *Humanities and Social Sciences Communications, 9,* 22.

Vuong, Q.-H., Nguyen, M.-H., & Le, T.-T. (2021). *A mindsponge-based investigation into the psycho-religious mechanism behind suicide attacks.* De Gruyter / Sciendo.

Wang, C., Lu, H., Zhang, J., He, K., & Huan, X. (2016). Macro-process of past plant subsistence from the Upper Paleolithic to Middle Neolithic in China: a quantitative analysis of multi-archaeobotanical data. *PLoS One, 11*(2), e0148136.

Watson, P. (2007). *Ideas: a history of thought and invention, from fire to Freud.* HarperPerennial.

Weiss, E., Kislev, M. E., Simchoni, O., & Nadel, D. (2004). Small-grained wild grasses as staple food at the 23 000-year-old site of Ohalo II, Israel. *Economic Botany, 58,* S125-S134.

Boat

©2021 Dam Thu Ha

Chapter 6:
A new theory of serendipity

Quan-Hoang Vuong, Tam-Tri Le, Quy Khuc, Minh-Hoang Nguyen

❧ • ❦

This chapter integrates major concepts presented in the preceding chapters into a new theory of serendipity. We formulate a framework that incorporates three aspects of serendipity: its conditionality, its nature as a survival skill, and its role in an information process incorporating the mindsponge mechanism and the 3D principles of creativity. We provide an integrated model for the causes and conditions of serendipity.

❧ • ❦

6.1. Distinctions with prior literature

In chapter 2, we have presented and discussed notable models, theories, and frameworks being introduced in previous studies to explain the serendipity process (André et al., 2009; Copeland, 2019; Cunha, 2005; Cunha et al., 2010; De Rond, 2014; Lawley & Tompkins, 2011; Makri & Blandford, 2012; McCay-Peet & Toms, 2010; McCay-Peet & Toms, 2015; Mendonça et al., 2008; Merton & Barber, 2004; Rubin et al., 2011). How is our new theory of serendipity different from previously proposed models, theories, and frameworks?

The greatest distinction is that we ask questions different from what they asked. The main questions asked in previous studies are:

1) What are the facets of serendipity?

https://doi.org/10.2478/9788366675865-012

2) How to increase the chance of encountering unexpected information and events that can lead to serendipity?
3) How to capitalize on such information and events and turn them into serendipity?

Meanwhile, our questions are:

- What is the nature of serendipity?
- What causes a serendipity phenomenon to occur?
- How can we improve the chance of having a serendipity strike?

Such questions lead us to develop a new theory of serendipity. This theory presents three main notions that correspond to the three questions stated above:

1) Serendipity is a conditional process.
2) Survival desires induce serendipity by creating goals (asking questions) and initiating the information-seeking and filtering process.
3) Improving the information recognition, evaluation, and connection processes will increase the chance of having a serendipity strike (answer the asked question).

Chapter 3 provides detailed explanations of the conditionality of the serendipity process, while Chapter 4 describes how serendipity is initiated from the survival instinct in terms of both natural and social contexts. This chapter aims to integrate the contents provided in Chapters 3 and 4 with the 3D framework of making creativity and the *mindsponge* mechanism to create a brand-new theory of serendipity. The new theory's three main notions are also clearly explained subsequently.

6.2. Mindsponge mechanism and 3D information process frameworks

Before delving into the framework of the new theory, it is worth reviewing some basic components and structures of the 3D framework of making creativity and the mindsponge mechanism.

• *3D information process of creativity*

The 3D information process of creativity is a conceptual framework that aims to use information and information processing to demonstrate how creativity can be made. The simplified 3D information process of creativity contains three main blocks: 1) an input block (or 'creative quantum' block), 2) a creativity processing block, and 3) an innovation outcomes block (Vuong & Napier, 2015; Vuong et al., 2022). Despite being shown as separate elements of the process, these blocks are so seamlessly and closely connected that separating them is almost impossible. Moreover, "3D" in the process's name stands for three disciplines proposed by Napier and Nilsson (2008) that have to be activated throughout the process:

• Being the best expertise within the discipline;
• Connecting the best expertise out of the discipline with the existing one;
• Following a disciplined process of employing methods of creativity strictly until the insights/innovations are generated.

The first block – input block – displays the filtering or assessment of inputs that enter the information process. Data (or quantifiable facts), information (or qualitative evidence, events that are less quantifiable and tangible), and 'primitive' insights (or initial connections between or from the first two types) are at least three types of the input. Although these inputs have some different characteristics, they can be treated as information in general throughout the information processing process. The information can come from various sources, including knowledge and experience stored in memory and observation from the external environment. When information enters the filtering system, it is evaluated, connected, compared, and used for thinking based on the individual's desire, pre-imagination, knowledge, skills, and disciplines for generating useful insights (or creative quanta) for the creativity processing block. During the filtering processes, "garbage" information (or information perceived as no or little value for the creativity-making process) is excluded for energy conserving. The information absorption and ejection mechanism can be explained by the mindsponge mechanism that will be mentioned below.

After the useful insights are generated, they enter the creativity processing block with some aspects that support a creative process. This process is a disciplined integrating process in which the individual incorporates inputs and a set of techniques and methods to generate creative outcomes and innovations. During the course, additional useful insights (or creative quanta) can be generated and inserted to aid the process of generating creative outcomes and innovations. In other words, disciplined creativity process block continuously incorporates useful insights generated from the input block until creative outcomes are achieved (in other words - arriving at the innovation outcomes block). The 'Aha! Moment' and serendipity also facilitate this process. An "Aha! Moment" is defined as the sudden awareness of a problem's solution or understanding an idea, which involves gathering, absorbing, and sorting information before using common techniques to spark new ideas, and then checking their generalizability (Berkun, 2010; Napier, 2010; Napier et al., 2009; Wallas, 1926). Although theoretically, when an outcome is obtained, the process will stop, that given outcome can still be later employed as a piece of information for another creativity-making process.

- *Mindsponge mechanism*

The mindsponge mechanism is first proposed by Vuong (2016) to describe the information process of an individual. The term "mindsponge" derives from the metaphor that the information process is analogized to a sponge that can squeeze out "garbage" or waning values and absorb new compatible values. According to Vuong & Napier (2015), a mindsponge consists of five main components: 1) mindset, 2) comfort zone (or buffer zone), 3) multi-filtering system, 4) cultural and ideological setting (external environment), and 5) cultural values (or information). It is assumed that each person has a mindset (or a set of core values) that influences their attitudes and behaviors. A person also uses core values as benchmarks explicitly or implicitly to make judgments on the usefulness and compatibility (in relation to one's current mindset) of information during the multi-filtering process (Nguyen et al., 2021; Nguyen & Vuong, 2021; Vuong et al., 2021a; Vuong et al., 2021b).

The cultural and ideological settings (or external environment) are where information comes from. When information is absorbed into the mind, the multi-filtering system kicks in to conduct evaluations. Two main functions of the multi-filtering system are making subjective cost-benefit judgments of the information (through the 3D multi-filtering process of creativity and inductive attitude) and evaluating the reliability of the information (through trust evaluators). If a piece of information is perceived as beneficial (positive net value), it will be allowed to get closer into the mindset; if it is perceived to be costly (negative net value), it will be ejected. However, if the mind cannot clearly determine whether the information is beneficial or not, it will temporarily keep the information in the comfort zone for later assessment. The closer the information is to the mindset, the more stringent the filtering process will become.

6.3. Serendipity: the cause and conditions

The theory of serendipity that we will present here is not built from scratch, but it is also grounded from other important works in the literature (Foster & Ford, 2003; Makri et al., 2014; McBirnie, 2008; Merton & Barber, 2004; Roberts, 1989; Rubin et al., 2011) and the framework proposed by one of the co-authors of this chapter and his colleague (Napier & Vuong, 2013). In the previous study, Napier and Vuong (2013) defined serendipity as "an ability (that can be developed) to notice, evaluate, and take advantage of unexpected information better or faster than competitors." Besides the unexpectedness, the new framework assumes that conditionality is another nature of serendipity (see Chapter 3 for more details), and the survival instincts of humans cause this conditionality (see Chapters 4 and 5 for more details). Thus, our theory defines serendipity as an ability to notice, evaluate, and take advantage of unexpected information for survival purposes (both natural and social), of which the outcome and success rate are conditional on the individual (or organizational) mindset and environment (see Figure 6.1). It should be noted that all events and phenomena will be treated as information when being observed by a person. Thus, by "unexpected information", we also refer to information directly derived from unexpected events and phenomena. This section focuses on explaining why serendipity's outcomes and success rates are conditional on the mindset and the environment.

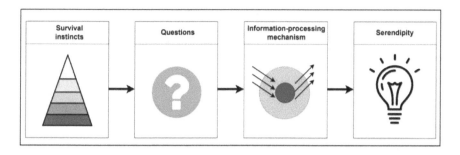

Figure 6.1: Causes and conditions of serendipity

For serendipity to happen, in most cases, it is required that a person has to be initially able to notice and recognize the potential value of the unexpected information, event, or phenomenon. It is clear that without the ability to notice and recognize the potential value of the unexpected information, serendipity will be unlikely to happen as the unexpected information will be quickly ejected from the mind.

The question is:

- **How can a person give value to a piece of information and decide to keep or reject it?**

This question can be explained by the 3D information process of creativity and the mindsponge information-processing mechanism. When a piece of information enters the mind, the multi-filtering process (or creative quantum) kicks in to evaluate, compare, and connect it with existing information in the mindset, comfort zone, and other new information absorbed from the environment simultaneously for judging the value of the given piece of information. A mindset is a collection of a person's core values (or highly trusted values/information). It is worth noting that the mindset does not have a clear boundary but rather, contained values are trusted (accepted) to certain degrees. In many cases, knowledge, insights, and skills within a person's discipline can be considered components of the core values, while knowledge and insights taken out of a person's discipline can be considered information from the environment. In other words, the process of recognizing and evaluating the value of the unexpected information requires the best expertise within a person's discipline (e.g., knowledge, insights, skills) and the ability to connect them with the best expertise out of the discipline (e.g., information from the environment, information from new sources/disciplines). Sometimes, the recognition and evaluation processes take a substantial amount of time, so a disciplined process of consistently employing the best of within-discipline and out-of-discipline information is also required.

During this process, the integration and differentiation of information happen simultaneously (Levy et al., 2007). While the integration process integrates, synthesizes, and incorporates information compatible with the core values, the differentiation process gauges the difference between the absorbed information from the environment and existing values in the mindset to evaluate the costs and benefits of accepting or rejecting the absorbing information. The cost-benefit judgment is mainly driven by the mindset because a mindset is a collection of a person's core values (or highly trusted values/information). In contrast, other emerging information has not yet been fully evaluated (having low levels of trust). However, in some cases, the existing information in the mindset can be ejected and replaced by new competing information if the newly absorbed information is perceived to be more beneficial.

For this reason, persons with distinct mindsets and being in distinct environments will value information (or representative of a thing or phenomenon) differently, and not all the pieces of information we observe every day (including those that are unexpected) are equally treated. Some will be subjectively favored more than others. In the case of Dr. Vuong, as presented in Chapter 3, he was interested in birds and bird nests, so he was inclined to absorb information related to birds and bird nests by attributing special value to them. However, without the information about the incident of his classmate Hưng and the beautiful illustration of birds in the textbook, he would probably not have been keen on birds as much. Another example is that a dog lover (a person with a mindset of favoring dogs) will attribute far more value to information related to dogs compared to a non-dog-lover.

Nevertheless, there will be fewer people with mindsets of favoring dogs if no dogs exist in their observable surroundings or if dogs in their region aggressively attack people. Following this way of reasoning, it is plausible to say that whether an unexpected piece of information is perceived to be valuable or not is conditional on the person's mindset (a set of core values or highly trusted information) and observed information from the environment. Another question is:

- **What forms the mindset?**

We do not know for sure what forms one's mindset. Yet, we advocate that the survival demands of humans heavily influence the mindset because, without these demands, humans would have gone extinct. Speaking differently, a person's mindset is a mental construct that exists with the purpose of meeting the survival demands of humans in response to the environment. Such demands include both natural and social survival demands. Elaboration on these survival demands is presented in Chapters 4 and 5. Here, we only provide brief explanations for each type of survival. While the definition of natural survival demand is relatively direct and tangible, that of social survival demand is less direct and more abstract. Natural survival demand is defined as the desire to prolong a physical existence (applied to both individual and collective levels). Social survival demand is defined as a desire to become the "fittest" in social contexts, with two main properties. The first property is the desire to acquire competitive advantages, mostly in resource-limited environments; the second property is the desire to prolong the person's social and mental constructs (e.g., identity, ideology, and possessions).

One's perceived existential threats (natural or social) are distinct based on particular situations, so their survival demands vary accordingly. Five types of motivations in Maslow's well-known hierarchy of needs are typical representations of a person's survival demands (Maslow, 1943; Maslow, 1981). Maslow classifies humans' needs into five levels: 1) physiological needs, 2) safety needs, 3) love/belongingness desires, 4) esteem desires, and 5) self-actualization desires. The former two levels are more driven by natural survival demands. In comparison, the latter three levels are more driven by social survival demands (see more details in Chapter 5).

When people have a demand, they need the information to determine the solution to meet their demand. Asking questions, implicitly or explicitly, is a human act of seeking information from both the memory (e.g., knowledge, insights, skills) and the external environment to meet their need for information. Suppose the need grows to a certain level. In that case, it will influence the mindset to internalize the necessity to satisfy the demand and prioritize (or give more perceived usefulness to) information that helps answer the question. The persistent internalization will eventually result in the institutionalization of special interest for that particular demand. Perhaps, one's mindset is formed through these internalization and institutionalization processes and becomes the conditions for later serendipity moments.

For example, in Dr. Vuong's story, he was amazed by his friend's "power of controlling" wild birds – a typical human desire for strength that reflects survival purposes – but he could not imitate his friend. This desire had laid a strong impression in his mind and substantially increased his demands for bird-related information. His questions of what natural birds and bird nests look like were representatives of such demands. Over time, the reinforcement of this desire helps cultivate his love for nature in general and birds in particular. Moreover, as Dr. Vuong is a researcher and philosopher, he wants to improve his skills, knowledge, and wisdom and convey his ideology through scientific works, theories, and principles. Gradually, these needs institutionalized his desire to generate "soul-touching" research in his mindset, which is an abstract kind of social survival demand. Both his love for nature and desire to produce valuable works were the conditions leading to the serendipity outcomes (e.g., the semi-conducting principle) when he recognized the value of the unexpected information (the birds drinking wastewater from the air conditioner).

As serendipity is a survival skill of humans, its outcomes are not always meaningful but may also be mediocre or mundane, depending on individuals and the situations. Humans have various kinds of survival demands, from physiological needs to self-actualization, so serendipity moments also appear in our daily life in numerous forms. It is just that we do not normally refer to them as serendipity phenomena. For instance, when a man is hungry after a long tiring working day and has no food left at home, he wonders what to eat. On the way home, suddenly, he can notice the smell of toasted garlic bread from a nearby bakery and decides to buy some bread for dinner. The serendipity outcome here is the man's solution for his hunger.

Another example is that a single boy accidentally bumps into a beautiful girl on the street. He decides to ask for the girl's contact and tries his best to capitalize on this incident to flirt with the girl. This is a disciplined process, during which the boy has to employ the best of his within-discipline knowledge, skills, and insights as well as look for the best of out-of-discipline resources (e.g., advice from friends, information on the internet). Eventually, they successfully become a couple and later get married. The marriage is an outcome of serendipity that creates a great value for both the boy and girl and helps meet their desire for love, belongingness. Furthermore, it may also meet their desire to have heirs. Although these examples focus on mundane events, they are also based on the mechanism of serendipity.

Nevertheless, what we mainly discuss in this book is serendipity that can lead to great values on collective levels and contribute to the advancement of human civilization (e.g., major innovations).

- **So, how can great outcomes of serendipity be created?**

Whether the outcomes of serendipity are great, mediocre, or mundane is conditional on the mindset and environment (Vuong, 2018). Regarding mindset, the first condition for the greatness of serendipity's outcomes is the "greatness" of the question being asked, or more specifically, the person's needs. To elaborate, one with mediocre or mundane priorities (e.g., mostly to satisfy physiological needs) will favor information related or analogous to those priorities. This makes them obtain less appropriate conditions and less capable of noticing and taking advantage of unexpected information for generating great innovative outcomes. Whereas, one with desires for something collectively valuable, meaningful, and soul-touching will be more likely to accumulate and attain sufficient conditions and abilities to notice greater values and take advantage of unexpected information for generating great innovative outcomes (the soul-touching concept is elaborated in Chapter 8). This is why, based on similar unexpected information, some people's serendipity process outcomes (providing survival skills) are mundane, but those of others are great.

The greater the outcomes, the higher abilities and conditions the serendipity process requires. Having a big question or desire for something great in mind is necessary but not enough. Great serendipity outcomes require a person's or organization's best expertise within discipline, best expertise out of discipline, and disciplined process to be achieved. However, anything has its limits. If a person's or organization's limits are reached, but the value of serendipity's outcomes has not been fully capitalized, the outcome's greatness will be diminished. The serendipity gained and lost in the case of floppy-eared-rabbit discovery is a prime example (see more details in Chapter 9). Apart from the outcome's greatness, these limits also constrain the success rate of the serendipity process. Due to its length, the conditions influencing serendipity success probability will be described further in a separate chapter, specifically, Chapter 7.

One's priorities do not naturally emerge from the mindset but come from interactions with the external environment. Two main types of information in the environment can help increase the serendipity encounter chance as well as the greatness of serendipity outcomes:

1) navigational information, and
2) useful information for the serendipity process.

Navigational information is the type of information that navigates people toward great goals by helping cultivate good core values (e.g., compassion, kindness, gratefulness, eco-surplus culture, work ethic) and avoid bad core values (e.g., laziness, greedy, eco-deficit culture, extreme materialism). Useful information is the type of information that helps prepare knowledge background and facilitates the capitalization of unexpected information. More specifically, navigational information can be deemed inputs for answering "what to do" questions. In contrast, useful information can be deemed inputs for answering "how to do it." We will present more details about the roles of these two kinds of information and how to build an environment that helps nurture mindset and maximize the success rate for serendipity with great outcomes in Chapter 10.

Chapter references

André, P., Schraefel, M., Teevan, J., & Dumais, S. T. (2009). Discovery is never by chance: designing for (un) serendipity. *Proceedings of the Seventh ACM Conference on Creativity and Cognition*, 305-314.

Berkun, S. (2010). *The myths of innovation*. O'Reilly.

Copeland, S. (2019). On serendipity in science: discovery at the intersection of chance and wisdom. *Synthese, 196*(6), 2385-2406.

Cunha, M. P. (2005). Serendipity: why some organizations are luckier than others. *FEUNL Working Paper Series, 472.*

Cunha, M. P. E., Clegg, S. R., & Mendonça, S. (2010). On serendipity and organizing. *European Management Journal, 28*(5), 319-330.

De Rond, M. (2014). The structure of serendipity. *Culture and Organization, 20*(5), 342-358.

Foster, A., & Ford, N. (2003). Serendipity and information seeking: an empirical study. *Journal of Documentation, 59*(3), 321-340.

Lawley, J., & Tompkins, P. (2011). *Maximising serendipity: The art of recognising and fostering unexpected potential - A systemic approach to change*. The Clean Collection. Retrieved from (December 31, 2021) https://cleanlanguage.co.uk/articles/articles/224/1/Maximising-Serendipity/Page1.html

Levy, O., Beechler, S., Taylor, S., & Boyacigiller, N. A. (2007). What we talk about when we talk about 'global mindset': Managerial cognition in multinational corporations. *Journal of International Business Studies, 38*(2), 231-258.

Makri, S., & Blandford, A. (2012). Coming across information serendipitously–Part 1: A process model. *Journal of Documentation, 68*(5), 684-705.

Makri, S., Blandford, A., Woods, M., Sharples, S., & Maxwell, D. (2014). "Making my own luck": Serendipity strategies and how to support them in digital information environments. *Journal of the Association for Information Science and Technology, 65*(11), 2179-2194.

Maslow, A. H. (1943). A theory of human motivation. *Psychological Review, 50*(4), 370-396.

Maslow, A. H. (1981). *Motivation and personality*. Prabhat Prakashan.

McBirnie, A. (2008). Seeking serendipity: the paradox of control. *Aslib Proceedings, 60*(6), 600-618.

McCay-Peet, L., & Toms, E. G. (2010). The process of serendipity in knowledge work. *Proceedings of the Third Symposium on Information Interaction in Context*, 377-382.

McCay-Peet, L., & Toms, E. G. (2015). Investigating serendipity: How it unfolds and what may influence it. *Journal of the Association for Information Science and Technology, 66*(7), 1463-1476.

Mendonça, S., Cunha, M., & Clegg, S. R. (2008). Unsought innovation: serendipity in organizations. Entrepreneurship and Innovation—Organizations, Institutions, Systems and Regions Conference, Copenhagen.

Merton, R. K., & Barber, E. (2004). *The travels and adventures of serendipity: a study in sociological semantics and the sociology of science*. Princeton University Press.

Napier, N. K. (2010). *Insight: encouraging Aha! moments for organizational success*. Praeger.

Napier, N. K., & Nilsson, M. (2008). *The creative discipline: mastering the art and science of innovation*. Praeger.

Napier, N. K., Bahnson, P. R., Glen, R., Maille, C. J., Smith, K., & White, H. (2009). When "Aha moments" make all the difference. *Journal of Management Inquiry, 18*(1), 64-76.

Napier, N., & Vuong, Q. H. (2013). Serendipity as a strategic advantage? In T. Wilkinson (Ed.), *Strategic management in the 21st century* (pp. 175-199). Praeger/ABC-Clio.

Nguyen, M.-H., & Vuong, Q.-H. (2021). Evaluation of the Aichi Biodiversity Targets: The international collaboration trilemma in interdisciplinary research. *Pacific Conservation Biology*.

Nguyen, M.-H., Le, T.-T., Nguyen, H.-K. T., Ho, M.-T., Nguyen, H. T. T., & Vuong, Q.-H. (2021). Alice in Suicideland: Exploring the suicidal ideation mechanism through the sense of connectedness and help-seeking behaviors. *International Journal of Environmental Research and Public Health, 18*(7), 3681.

Roberts, R. M. (1989). *Serendipity: accidental discoveries in science*. Wiley.

Rubin, V. L., Burkell, J., & Quan-Haase, A. (2011). Facets of serendipity in everyday chance encounters: a grounded theory approach to blog analysis. *Information Research, 16*(3), 488.

Vuong, Q. H. (2016). Global mindset as the integration of emerging socio-cultural values through mindsponge processes: A transition economy perspective. In J. Kuada (Ed.), *Global mindsets: exploration and perspectives* (pp. 109-126). Routledge.

Vuong, Q. H., & Napier, N. K. (2014). Making creativity: the value of multiple filters in the innovation process. *International Journal of Transitions and Innovation Systems, 3*(4), 294-327.

Vuong, Q. H., & Napier, N. K. (2015). Acculturation and global mindsponge: an emerging market perspective. *International Journal of Intercultural Relations, 49*, 354-367.

Vuong, Q.-H. (2018). The (ir)rational consideration of the cost of science in transition economies. *Nature Human Behaviour, 2*, 5.

Vuong, Q.-H., et al. (2022). Covid-19 vaccines production and societal immunization under the serendipity-mindsponge-3D knowledge management theory and conceptual framework. *Humanities and Social Sciences Communications, 9*, 22.

Vuong, Q.-H., Nguyen, M.-H., & Le, T.-T. (2021a). *A mindsponge-based investigation into the psycho-religious mechanism behind suicide attacks*. De Gruyter / Sciendo.

Vuong, Q.-H., Nguyen, M.-H., & Le, T.-T. (2021b). Home scholarly culture, book selection reason, and academic performance: Pathways to book reading interest among secondary school students. *European Journal of Investigation in Health, Psychology and Education, 11*(2), 468-495.

Wallas, G. (1926). *The Art of Thought*. Jonathan Cape.

Kingfisher

©2017 Bui Quang Khiem

Chapter 7:
Conditions for improving serendipity encounter and attainment probability

Minh-Hoang Nguyen

While we cannot ensure the occurrence of serendipity due to its nature of unexpectedness, we can try to prepare the optimal conditions to improve the possibility. This chapter first describes two types of unexpected information: within or from beyond one's perceivable range. Next, we describe four stages of the serendipity attainment process: navigation, noticing, evaluation, and implementation. On this basis, we discuss six scenarios in the order of serendipity encounter and attainment probability, which are determined by information availability in the environment and the mindset in terms of information processing. The serendipity attainment process has a higher success rate when acquiring precise navigation and employing the 3D principles of creativity (best expertise within discipline, the best expertise out of discipline, and discipline process).

7.1. What is unexpectedness?

In the previous chapter, we presented the nature of serendipity and what causes a serendipity phenomenon to appear. This chapter will clarify the process leading to serendipity outcomes by explaining the conditions that can help increase the success probability of serendipity. This section, in other words, aims to explain how to improve the ability

https://doi.org/10.2478/9788366675865-013

to notice, evaluate, and take advantage of unexpected information for generating serendipity outcomes.

To begin with, we need to clarify the concept of "unexpectedness" in the context of serendipity and make some premises. According to the Oxford dictionary, unexpectedness is when something surprises you because you were not expecting it. Here, we would like to refer to unexpectedness as a person's subjective perceptions of a certain event but not the objective existence of the event itself (Nguyen, 2021). Former works on serendipity models and processes also shared analogous viewpoints. For example, Lawley and Tompkins (2011) suggest that the serendipity process is a perceptual process that comprises six major components, including the unexpected event. Meanwhile, McCay-Peet and Toms (2015)'s model mentions the perception of serendipity as one out of six major elements of the serendipity process. They refer to the perception of serendipity as an experience "understood or regarded to be serendipitous based on awareness of its trigger, connection, valuable outcome, and unexpected thread."

The unexpected moment happens when a person subjectively expects it not to happen or when a person first perceives novel information they have no reference in mind. Therefore, there can be two circumstances.

- **Unexpectedness from within the perceivable range**: In the first circumstance, the thing/event that surprises a person has already existed or occurred within that person's perceivable range for a certain period, but that person does not notice or perceive its existence/occurrence. For some reason, the person becomes aware of that thing/event and considers it unexpected. By saying perceivable range, we mean the physical range (or environment) within which a person can see, hear, or become aware of something through the senses. For instance, on the way from home to school or office, the surrounding scenes, sounds, and smells are things/events that can be perceived; After a long walk, the person feels surprised when he/she recognizes that the person walking alongside for a while is their friend. Another example is that many people may listen to the Twinkle Twinkle Little Star and ABC songs, but they may not immediately recognize that they have the same tune.

- **Unexpectedness from beyond the perceivable range**: In the second circumstance, the thing/event that surprises a person does not exist or occur within the past or current perceivable range of that person but comes from outside of the perceivable range. A person may not intentionally seek that information. Still, due to the changes in the environment, a thing/event suddenly appears or occurs within the person's perceivable range and makes them surprised. For instance, on the way from home or to school or office, one unexpectedly runs into their friend who walks out of a nearby restaurant.

These two circumstances are derived from two fundamental assumptions about human physical and mental capacities. The first assumption is that a person's mental capacity has a certain limit, so they cannot perceive, evaluate, and absorb all the information from their perceivable range. For example, a person cannot see all the details in a complex illustration but can solely focus on a specific part of the illustration at a time; Where's Wally – a British animated series of children's puzzle books created by an English illustrator Martin Handford – is a prime example. The second assumption is that a person's physical capacity has a certain limit, so they cannot receive information out of their perceivable range. For example, one cannot see things/events that exist or occur without their eyesight; a person cannot directly see the Eiffel Tower in France while standing in front of the Washington Monument in the United States.

7.2. Serendipity outcome attainment process

In Chapter 6, serendipity has been defined as an ability to notice, evaluate, and take advantage of unexpected information for survival demands (both natural and social), of which its outcome and success rate are conditional on the individual mindset and environment. Based on this definition, the 3D information process of creativity (Vuong et al., 2022; Vuong & Napier, 2014), mindsponge mechanism (Vuong & Napier, 2015; Vuong, 2016), and serendipity framework of Napier and Vuong (2013), we propose that there are four major stages in the serendipity outcome attainment process: 1) navigation, 2) noticing, 3) evaluation, and 4) implementation. The success probability of attaining a serendipity outcome is dependent on each stage of the process, and each stage is conditional on not only a person's or organization's mindset but also the environment. Analogous to the creativity-making process, one must possess the proactive, self-motivated, self-reliant, and risk-taking attitude to initiate the serendipity process (Vuong, 2019; Vuong & Napier, 2014). The more a person's or organization's mindset follows the 3D principles (the best within the discipline, the best out of discipline, and disciplined process) of the 3D information process, the higher probability of a serendipity outcome. Meanwhile, if a person or organization receives information from an environment rich in useful and navigational information, they will have higher chances of attaining serendipity outcomes.

- **Navigation**

We begin with the assumption that any person or organization has certain survival instincts (either social or natural). Such instincts heavily influence their mindset (a set of core values) and subsequently affect thinking, affection, attitudes, and behaviors. It should be noted that core values in the mindset are not static but continuously updated based on experience (information about the past), observation (information at the moment), and imagination (information about the future). One's survival instincts arise when one perceives existential threats based on the information from the environment and the mind. The survival instincts drive them to demand information to solve the problem.

To attain the required information, a person or organization has to navigate the environments holding a large amount of information helpful for their needs. One of the fundamental ways to navigate is to formulate questions. Choosing an appropriate direction (or making an appropriate question) can greatly improve the chance of encountering useful information to solve their problem. This is in line with Thagard and Croft's (1999) viewpoint that serendipity is not simply blindly stumbling on important phenomena or simple trials and waiting for the luck to come, but it requires highly insightful questions and searching for solutions. An environment with a lot of information that helps a person or organization navigate can also facilitate their navigational process.

Whether a person or an organization can choose an appropriate direction (or make an appropriate question) or not depends largely on their abilities to identify useful insights and (or) primitive solutions available (within-discipline) as well as their abilities to connect them with information beyond normally perceived boundaries from the environment (out-of-discipline). Therefore, to maximize the success rate of attaining serendipity outcomes, using the best information within one's discipline and connecting the best information out of discipline are required. Furthermore, a disciplined process is also necessary, as identifying and connecting the most useful information from the mindset and environment takes time and effort to be completed.

- **Noticing**

There are two conditions for a person or organization to notice unexpected information or useful information that helps capitalize the unexpected information. First, the information must be available within the perceivable range of a person or an organization. Second, a person or an organization must be able to perceive and quickly recognize the potential value of the information, or at least enough for the information to be stored in the buffer zone for later assessment. While the first condition cannot be controlled, the 3D principles can be employed to improve the second condition and increase the success rate of serendipity attainment.

The likelihood of perceiving information from the environment can be improved by actively and constantly observing the environment. A person's perceivable range is likened to a radar; the longer it is turned on, the more likely it can catch useful information. Holding sufficient experience, knowledge, wisdom, and abilities to process and connect information observed from the environment are required to detect the potential usefulness of the information more quickly and accurately. Openness to new information (which has not been encountered before) or conflicting information is also important to the noticing process. Although one can perceive or observe objectively useful information without sufficient expertise and openness, they will likely exclude them subjectively, leading to serendipity lost scenarios. In other words, to notice information that can lead to valuable discovery, it is necessary to acquire a disciplined preparedness. Like Louis Pasteur rightly put it: "*Dans les champs de l'observation le hasard ne favorise que les esprits prepares*" [In the fields of observation, chance favors only the prepared mind].

- **Evaluation or verification**

Systematic evaluation is the third stage for successfully taking advantage of unexpected information. During this stage, a more analytical and rigorous assessment of the unexpected information is conducted to confirm the anticipated opportunity from the unexpected information, evaluate the possibility and risks of the anticipated opportunity, identify influential factors, and plan implementation methods. Sometimes, the systematic evaluation also prevents one from missing additional values that cannot be detected in the first place when noticing the unexpected information. The systematic evaluation process also needs the involvement of a person or an organization's best expertise within the discipline (e.g., experience, knowledge, wisdom, resources), best expertise out of discipline (e.g., new information, new knowledge, new resources), and disciplined process (e.g., perseverance) of applying expertise for maximizing the success probability serendipity process and reducing risks. Connecting existing information with new ones can support a person or an organization in recognizing more values (e.g., opportunities) that can be capitalized from the unexpected information compared to when it was first noticed.

During the evaluation process, a person or organization has to absorb a great amount of information from the environment to improve their knowledge, wisdom, and analytical abilities. Hence, an environment rich in useful information will enhance the assessment precision and implementation effectiveness. In contrast, if useful information in the environment is not available, one needs to seek information from other environments (or information sources); if information in the environment is chaotic, one has to constantly employ their expertise to differentiate, organize, and exclude "garbage" values from the mindset, which will hinder the serendipity attainment process. Here, physical resources can also be considered "useful information" because the serendipity process happens perceptually.

- **Implementation**

Finally, implementation is indispensable for taking advantage of unexpected information and satisfying survival demands. One's actions in this stage are contingent on their mindset and environment. They require one's greatest experience, knowledge, wisdom, and abilities (e.g., skills, thinking ability, resources) and new resources, new information, and knowledge from the environment to be successful. A person or organization must follow a disciplined process until the outcomes are accomplished. Otherwise, formerly spent times, efforts, and resources will be wasted. Many sub-serendipity processes may happen across the main serendipity process and add more chance to attaining the main serendipity outcome.

7.3. Conditions for improving the probability of serendipity encounter and attainment

The 3D information process of creativity and the mindsponge mechanism are core components of the serendipity process. Based on these two mechanisms, we indicate five major conditions that need to be met in all four stages of the serendipity process to increase the success probability. They include:

1) availability of information,

2) appropriate direction,
3) disciplined process,
4) sufficient openness and observing abilities,
5) sufficient experience, knowledge, wisdom, and abilities.

These five conditions are visualized into five scenarios in Figure 7.1 for easier interpretation. For the same reason, several examples are provided in the explanation. The sixth scenario shows when serendipity outcomes are achieved in both normal and delayed manners.

- **Scenario 1: Availability of information**

One of the most fundamental elements that determine the serendipity process's success probability is the existence of information in the environment around a person (or within the perceivable range). It should be noted that here we assume the information to be representative of physical objects (e.g., money, resources) when being absorbed into the human mind. One can perceive such information as "information particles" (Nguyen & Le, 2021; Nguyen et al., 2021; Vuong et al., 2021).

There are two main types of information in a serendipity process: navigational and useful information. Navigational information is any knowledge, events, wisdom, etc. that helps guide a person or an organization to desirable solutions in the decision-making process, while useful information is any knowledge, events, wisdom, etc., that are constructive towards a solution. Unexpected information can be either navigational or useful information. What makes a particular piece of unexpected information different from others is the subjective judgment of whether the information appears unexpectedly or not. Distinguishably, unexpected information has special subjective values for the person (or organization) in relation to a particular problem-solving process.

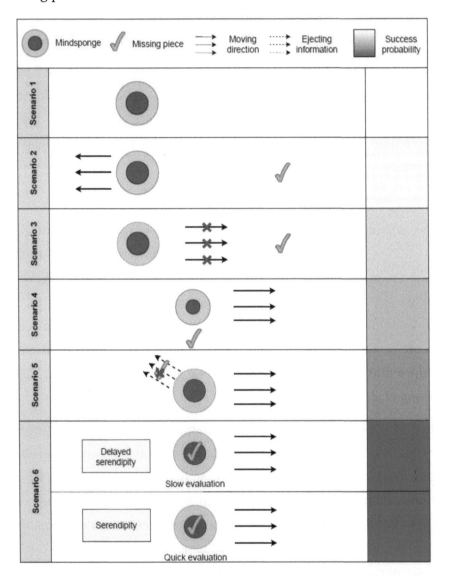

Figure 7.1: Conditions leading to serendipity outcome attainment

Regardless of its type, the information does not spontaneously appear first in mind, but it is something that a person has to perceive from the environment initially. Thus, it is plausible that without the existence of information in the environment (or perceivable range), a person can neither notice, evaluate, or take advantage of it. For instance, if sulfur did not exist, there would be no related discoveries or applications of that chemical element. And if there were no accidental discovery of "fire medicine" (or *huoyao*, 火药/火藥) by the Chinese Taoists on their quest for the elixir of life in the 9th century AD, gunpowder would not have appeared in China so early (Andrade, 2017; Chase, 2003). The first scenario in Figure 7.1 illustrates this circumstance.

- **Scenario 2: appropriate direction**

Each question/problem requires specific navigational and useful information to be answered/solved. Although unexpectedness means something surprising and cannot be foreseen, the chance of meeting a particular kind of information is objectively contingent on the environment. Each environment (or source of information) has its unique characteristics or holds a particular information set. In each set of information, there are various types of information, and each type of information has a particular density level. The density level can be high or low. For example, in some urban ecosystems, the density of concrete-building and human-related information are among the highest; in a protected areas related website, the density of plant-related and species-related information are among the highest; in a social research institute, the density of academic and social-sciences-related information (from books, researchers, students) are among the highest.

Thus, selecting an environment rich in the information necessary to answer a particular question or solve a particular problem will help increase the probability of meeting the unexpected information and sufficiently collect other information to capitalize on that unexpected information successfully. In other words, choosing the right environment will help a person or organization increase their chance to notice the important missing piece that can lead to a serendipity outcome. They have to navigate the environments that make it more accessible and likely to perceive the unexpected information ("missing piece") and other information facilitating its capitalization. For example, an anthropologist will have a higher probability of finding the unexpected "missing pieces" and other essential information for solving their problems in the field by observing human behaviors, cultures, and societies than by looking at mathematics formulas. A company only consulting with its staff members who have limited knowledge about the market expansion will be less likely to encounter serendipity on business opportunities than frequently consulting with market research experts. Scenario 2 in Figure 7.1 demonstrates the circumstance that a person or an organization is highly likely to fail to solve problems because of choosing the wrong direction.

The success of Starbucks is a typical example of choosing the right direction. Howard Schultz, the person who changed the business direction of Starbucks and turned it into a successful multinational company, found his crucial serendipity strike when he was sent to Milan in 1983. At the time, Italy could be considered the center of European coffee culture. We can clearly see that Schultz's decision to observe the local cafés there put him into a great environment for encountering the kind of information greatly helpful for his innovation purposes. Apparently, Starbucks's innovative business direction could not have been implemented had Starbuck decided not to give Schultz the opportunity or Schultz decided to spend more time only at the conference instead of going out to observe local cafés.

- **Scenario 3: disciplined process**

Besides being dependent on the state of information availability, serendipity's success rate is also conditional on a person's mindset – the best expertise within discipline, the best expertise out of discipline, and disciplined manner. We can set the direction of our action toward the environment that increases our chance to encounter information beneficial for our problem-solving tasks (including unexpected information), but we cannot know where and when we will catch such useful information and under which conditions because of the unexpectedness of serendipity. After selecting the right direction, a person or an organization has to keep a high level of perseverance for seeking information to increase their chance of encountering valuable unexpected information. The longer we persist with our rightly chosen direction, the higher chance we can encounter those "missing pieces", or the higher chance they will fall into our perceivable range. Even after successfully noticing the value of unexpected information, the serendipity outcomes cannot be achieved if a person or an organization does not implement subsequent actions to capitalize on the opportunities in a disciplined manner. The illustration of scenario 3 in Figure 7.1 demonstrates this circumstance.

It is important to note that the "rightly chosen direction" is dynamic in nature, which means that the direction can be right at first but can turn out to be wrong if some conditions are changed. A disciplined process can improve the chance of encountering valuable unexpected information and capitalize it. Still, if the process is heading astray, it will decrease the serendipity chance by wasting one's time, efforts, and resources. Therefore, a disciplined reflection process is also required to make sure one is not moving astray. For example, individuals' and enterprises' business directions must be reviewed and adjusted quickly to increase resilience and, perhaps, take advantage of the opportunities when an economic recession or global crisis (e.g., COVID-19 pandemic) suddenly happens (Schell et al., 2020).

- **Scenario 4: sufficient openness and observing abilities**

The second principle of the 3D information process of creativity is the ability to connect the best expertise out of discipline to find the optimal solution or answer. To connect, one has to absorb the information into the mind initially. Two elements that can hinder the absorption process are the limited perceivable range and the lack of open-mindedness (Cunha et al., 2010; Mendonça et al., 2008). The perceivable range can be deemed a person's or an organization's radar that collects accessible information. A poor perceivable range will result in a limited amount of information being absorbed, reducing the chance of noticing, evaluating, and capitalizing on valuable information (including unexpected ones). Lack of open-mindedness can be deemed the circumstance in which new information is more likely to be ejected due to the limited references within the mindset rather than stored in the buffer zone for later assessment.

Usually, a person or an organization has regular routines that it tends to follow every day. When following such routines, information within their perceivable range might not change too much, making the person or organization attain less chance to acknowledge unexpected information. Suppose one faces an impasse in answering a question or solving a problem for a long time. In that case, it is plausible that there is little unexpected and essential information that can help them answer the question or solve a problem in the information sources they are receiving from. A person can improve their perceivable range by optimizing their skills of collecting information (e.g., observation, reading, listening skills) and increasing their accessibility to more information sources (e.g., reading new books, observing new things, traveling to new places). For an organization, the perceivable range can be improved by hiring new experts, building an open environment for information exchange (e.g., holding conferences), conducting market research, etc. (De Rond, 2014; Dew, 2009; Mendonça et al., 2008). The serendipity case of Starbucks and Howard Schultz is a typical example of expanding their information perceivable range.

Any person or organization has a self-affirmation tendency, which is the likelihood of integrating values similar to their mindset (core values) and ejecting values opposing their mindset (Steele, 1988). Lack of openness will prevent a complete and effective assessment of new information (e.g., ideas, phenomena). Thus, even if one already observed certain information, they will still be likely to remove such information from their minds, especially if its unexpectedness is negatively judged.

- **Scenario 5: sufficient experience, knowledge, wisdom, and abilities**

The last principle in the 3D information process is the ability to employ the best expertise within one's discipline to identify insights for problem-solving. Because information processing is not static but rather a dynamic process, the condition is affected by the past condition and will influence the future condition. Thus, the sufficiency of experience, knowledge, wisdom, and abilities is seamlessly connected with all the stages and other conditions in the serendipity process. To elaborate, with sufficient experience, knowledge, wisdom, and abilities, one will be more likely to choose the right direction, notice, evaluate, and take advantage of valuable information, the benefits will subsequently improve their experience, knowledge, wisdom, abilities, and resources, increasing the success probability of later serendipity processes. On the opposite, without sufficient experience, knowledge, wisdom, and abilities, the effectiveness of navigation, noticing, evaluation, and implementation will be substantially reduced, mitigating the success probability of the serendipity process.

- **Scenario 6: Delayed and normal serendipity**

When all the five conditions listed above are ensured, a person or an organization has a very high chance to successfully notice, evaluate, and capitalize the value of unexpected information. In other words, serendipity outcomes are accomplished and result in strategic advantages for the person or organization (Napier & Vuong, 2013; Vuong, 2018). However, what is the distinctions between delayed and normal serendipity?

During the information processing process, a great number of information pieces are absorbed, ejected, and stored in mind simultaneously. Those stored in the buffer zone are information of which value cannot be justified as costly or beneficial at the moment, thus, sometimes making the recognition of unexpected information's value not always happen immediately. The evaluation can be delayed (McCay-Peet & Toms, 2015), similar to the incubation period suggested by McCay-Peet and Toms (2010). After a certain period, one's knowledge, wisdom, and abilities are sufficiently accumulated to notice, evaluate, and capitalize on unexpected information. Such unexpectedness can come from two places: the environment and the buffer zone. If the unexpected information is absorbed from the environment and helps one achieve a serendipity outcome, this circumstance can be considered a normal serendipity process. Suppose one finds a piece of information stored in mind (mostly in the buffer zone) for a long time, unexpected after a re-evaluation process or connecting it with newly observed information. In that case, this circumstance can be called a delayed serendipity process.

The conditions presented in this chapter are theoretically constructed based on the mindsponge mechanism and 3D information process of creativity so that they will need further validation. In Chapter 9, these conditions, together with the new theory proposed in Chapter 6, will be validated using the famous serendipity story of the floppy-eared-rabbit discovery (Barber & Fox, 1958), while the next chapter will clarify the concept of soul-touching and how it affects the greatness of serendipity outcomes.

Chapter references

Andrade, T. (2017). *The gunpowder age: China, military innovation, and the rise of the West in world history*. Princeton University Press.

Barber, B., & Fox, R. C. (1958). The case of the floppy-eared rabbits: An instance of serendipity gained and serendipity lost. *American Journal of Sociology, 64*(2), 128-136.

Chase, K. (2003). *Firearms: a global history to 1700*. Cambridge University Press.

Cunha, M. P. e., Clegg, S. R., & Mendonça, S. (2010). On serendipity and organizing. *European Management Journal, 28*(5), 319-330.

De Rond, M. (2014). The structure of serendipity. *Culture and Organization, 20*(5), 342-358.

Dew, N. (2009). Serendipity in entrepreneurship. *Organization Studies, 30*(7), 735-753.

Lawley, J., & Tompkins, P. (2011). *Maximising serendipity: The art of recognising and fostering unexpected potential - A systemic approach to change*. The Clean Collection. Retrieved from (December 31, 2021)

https://cleanlanguage.co.uk/articles/articles/224/1/Maximising
-Serendipity/Page1.html

McCay-Peet, L., & Toms, E. G. (2010). The process of serendipity in
knowledge work. *Proceedings of the Third Symposium on
Information Interaction in Context, 377–382.*

McCay-Peet, L., & Toms, E. G. (2015). Investigating serendipity: how
it unfolds and what may influence it. *Journal of the Association
for Information Science and Technology, 66(7), 1463-1476.*

Mendonça, S., Cunha, M., & Clegg, S. R. (2008). Unsought innovation:
serendipity in organizations. Entrepreneurship and
Innovation—Organizations, Institutions, Systems and Regions
Conference, Copenhagen.

Napier, N., & Vuong, Q. H. (2013). Serendipity as a strategic
advantage? In T. Wilkinson (Ed.), *Strategic management in the
21st century* (pp. 175-199). Praeger/ABC-Clio.

Nguyen, M.-H. (2021). Subjective spheres of influence: a perceptual
system beyond mindsponge. *PhilArchive.*
https://philarchive.org/rec/NGUSSO

Nguyen, M.-H., & Le, T.-T. (2021). Information particle. *OSF
Preprints.* https://osf.io/fgjpz

Nguyen, M.-H., Le, T.-T., Nguyen, H.-K. T., Ho, M.-T., Nguyen, H. T.
T., & Vuong, Q.-H. (2021). Alice in Suicideland: exploring the
suicidal ideation mechanism through the sense of
connectedness and help-seeking behaviors. *International
Journal of Environmental Research and Public Health, 18(7), 3681.*

Schell, D., Wang, M., & Huynh, T. L. D. (2020). This time is indeed
different: A study on global market reactions to public health
crisis. *Journal of Behavioral and Experimental Finance, 27, 100349.*

Steele, C. M. (1988). The psychology of self-affirmation: Sustaining the integrity of the self. In L. Berkowitz (Ed.), *Advances in experimental social psychology* (Vol. 21, pp. 261-302). Elsevier.

Thagard, P., & Croft, D. (1999). Scientific discovery and technological innovation: Ulcers, dinosaur extinction, and the programming language JAVA. In L. Magnani, N. J. Nersessian, & P. Thagard (Eds.), *Model-based reasoning in scientific discovery* (pp. 125-137). Kluwer Academic.

Vuong, Q. H. (2016). Global mindset as the integration of emerging socio-cultural values through mindsponge processes: A transition economy perspective. In J. Kuada (Ed.), *Global mindsets: exploration and perspectives* (pp. 109-126). Routledge.

Vuong, Q. H., & Napier, N. K. (2014). Making creativity: the value of multiple filters in the innovation process. *International Journal of Transitions and Innovation Systems, 3*(4), 294-327.

Vuong, Q.-H. (2018). The (ir)rational consideration of the cost of science in transition economies. *Nature Human Behaviour, 2,* 5.

Vuong, Q.-H. (2019). Breaking barriers in publishing demands a proactive attitude. *Nature Human Behaviour, 3,* 1034.

Vuong, Q.-H., & Napier, N. K. (2015). Acculturation and global mindsponge: an emerging market perspective. *International Journal of Intercultural Relations, 49,* 354-367.

Vuong, Q.-H., Le, T.-T., La, V.-P., Nguyen, T. T. H., Ho, M.-T., Khuc, Q., & Nguyen, M.-H. (2022). Covid-19 vaccines production and societal immunization under the serendipity-mindsponge-3D knowledge management theory and conceptual framework. *Humanities and Social Sciences Communications, 9,* 22.

Vuong, Q.-H., Nguyen, M.-H., & Le, T.-T. (2021). Home scholarly culture, book selection reason, and academic performance:

Pathways to book reading interest among secondary school students. *European Journal of Investigation in Health, Psychology and Education, 11*(2), 468-495.

Lighthouse

©2021 Dam Thu Ha

Chapter 8:
From soul-touching concept to serendipity greatness

Quan-Hoang Vuong

❧ • ☙

This chapter is dedicated to explaining the soul-touching concept and its relationship with serendipity outcomes. Based on my reflections on what I call soul-touching research in humanities and social sciences, I describe how the "soul factor" contributes to the greatness of serendipity outcomes.

❧ • ☙

8.1. Introduction

The ancient city of Megiddo likely conjures in us no images or geographical connection. Yet, this 7,000-year-old site in Israel is where the biblical legend of Armageddon – the last battle between the good and evil before the Day of Judgement – sprouted and fed our imagination of a lost great civilization or some historic battles. When I read a recent story about the decades-long excavation efforts at Megiddo (Robinson, 2020), I was struck by the image that, perhaps when Alexander the Great marched through this city, all of its historical significance had faded into oblivion. As a social scientist, this made me ponder the fate of our academic journey. If an ancient fallen city is remembered even by a few short biblical descriptions of its greatness, are we capable of conducting research with the same memorability?

https://doi.org/10.2478/9788366675865-014

We researchers in the humanities and social sciences, similar to the archaeologists but only less literally, are constantly digging through unknown dirt and even uncharted territories in hopes of finding "diamonds." Clearly, the search for self-actualization or self-empowerment is inherent in every researcher as our survival instincts, even as he or she may have started out in academia with the most mundane goal of publishing as many articles as possible. This process is arduous and time-consuming.

In previous chapters, we have attributed the serendipity outcomes' greatness to the desire to do something valuable, meaningful, and soul-touching. While valuable and meaningful things are understandable, what the desire to do something "soul-touching" be like? In this chapter, I will present more in-depth explanations about the soul-touching concept and its relationship with the greatness of serendipity outcomes using some reflections on my journey, one that I would call the quest for soul-touching research.

8.2. The soul-touching research: reflections on my experiences

One of the first things to remember is none of us is alone in this quest. As I looked back upon how the search for my self-defined "soul-touching" research took shape, I recalled a piece of advice (and encouragement) from my colleague, Prof. Nancy K. Napier, of Boise State University (https://nancyknapier.com/). In an email sent to me last year, she had written: "It [the soul factor] is absolutely the right reason to do hard work."

This "soul factor" is not an abstraction; it is about meeting at least three out of the following four criteria: (i) doing good work, (ii) learning a lot, (iii) working with good people, and (iv) having fun. As Prof. Napier and I agree, the factor emphasizes the importance of good teamwork, doing research with good people, and helping real people. For my colleague, with her 40+ years of research experience, projects that "touched her soul" were those that have genuine impacts, rather than just scoring points in academia.

It is not easy for a researcher in the humanities and social sciences to choose which of her/his works can be considered the most important. But the quest for research pinnacles will continue for those who want to advance and make meaningful contributions and seek to create impact (not impact factor!).

For me, it can be a manifestation of a journey to find soul-touching research. The searching process can help me answer such questions as: Who am I? Why was I born? What am I meant to do with my time? What is beautiful and valuable in my mind? What values can even transcend lifetimes?

'Normal' research projects tend to focus on data and techniques. Large datasets and fancy techniques with terrifying complexities are researchers' usual obsession. The researchers are under pressure, either self-imposed or from a "publish or perish" university climate, to produce striking results and impressive work acceptable to busy editors and precarious reviewers. For these research projects, it is understandable that researchers tend to forget the "soul factor" since they believe that what editors and reviewers think is of higher importance and relevance.

However, the "soul factor" is exactly what divides the world of research into the mediocre (including the good-looking and useless) and the great.

Undertaking great work demands time, energy, perseverance (following repeated failures) and can affect the researcher's health.

Economic concerns (e.g., cost-benefit analysis, optimal use of time, or the like) are non-existent when researchers pursue soul-touching projects. Due to such reasons, integrating the soul factor into research will greatly improve the greatness of serendipity outcomes (Vuong et al., 2022).

For me, the three following serendipitous projects manifest a soul-touching research journey.

- **Case no. 1: "Probabilities of destitution" have real faces**

As scientists, we may get tangled up in our own data and statistics, sometimes falsely putting the emphasis on a certain statistical significance test than on the real subjects involved in the test themselves. This misguided obsession not only takes away the "soul factor" of the research but also a researcher's own soul, if I dare say.

In a research project conducted in 2014 on the risk of Vietnamese patients falling into destitution because of financial burdens (Vuong, 2015), I spent hours getting to know the real faces and profiles of people affected by the shortfalls in government health care policies as well as their limited economic conditions in case of sickness. The documented patient Nguyen Thi Lan (in a small commune in the southern Kien Giang province) was one of the countless examples of families undergoing financial hardships when one member got sick. As I came face-to-face with real patients whose health withered away and lived poorer each day, pieces of my heart broke.

Researchers are so often intently focused on collecting as many surveys as possible that getting one's heart and soul out there to connect with and understand the respondents seems like the very last thing. This is not to say that the surveys were emotionally driven and subject to emotional biases. My point is to have soul-touching research, we as researchers should be able to resonate with the real individuals in our projects. For me, I was able to identify factors conventionally overlooked in this kind of research. For instance, low-income patients with serious conditions are unlikely to give high amounts of "thank-you money"—which may be a cultural norm in Vietnam—because they are already paying for high treatment costs and unaccountable out-of-pocket payments at the hospitals.

In this project, my outlook on healthcare research expanded and re-examined, giving rise to new ideas — precisely showing the "serendipity" at work.

- **Case no. 2: Ancient stories, like the "Lost City of Solomon," once unearthed properly, can be empowering**

A second project yielded the publication of an article on Three Teachings (Confucianism, Taoism, and Buddhism) and religious values in ages-old folktales (Vuong et al., 2018). And it did not materialize out of a vacuum.

Three hours for conceiving the main ideas while having coffee on a Lunar New Year holiday in 2018.

Two weeks of preparing data. One week of statistical analysis, including computer code writing. Three more weeks for writing the first draft, and finally about four months for submitting and revising the manuscript before editorial acceptance.

The research ideas came from three people who were all near 50 by the time they conceived the value of life, and all three have been deeply influenced by folktales in their childhoods. The 'permanent bank' of the memory (or sufficient knowledge and experience) served them well and activated the serendipity mechanism.

How the ideas percolated in this case strongly depended upon how comfortable one was with letting values of statistical measures permeate through the layers of religious details and teachings. It requires sufficient openness, experience and knowledge, and a disciplined process to make religious teaching and folktale details be quantified in an analyzable way.

Without these three elements, the research process could not have even started.

- **Case no. 3: When art meets data science...**

In 2019, as we lamented the poor conservation of historic architecture around Hanoi, we had a strange idea of learning about cultural evolution by using photos of old houses in downtown Hanoi (Vuong et al., 2019). Our coauthor Bui Quang Khiem began taking photos in 2012 (see Figure 8.1). I accompanied him on another Lunar New Year holiday in 2017, taking photos of some old streets. The project made its debut in September 2018, when we saw the light emitted from performing some innovative data modeling.

During the undertaking, we even had to write a new computer package using the R language for about four months (La & Vuong, 2019; Vuong, La, Nguyen, Ho, Tran, et al., 2020). The same serendipity mechanism has led us to stumble on an opportunity to make a new type of academic contribution: computing and graphics software package in R. Also, collecting data required us to write a web-based program that enabled respondents to evaluate the photos.

For me, this project epitomizes the seamless working of both the "soul factor" and serendipity

Figure 8.1: A linocut painting by Bui Quang Khiem examined during the undertaking of (Vuong et al., 2019).

8.3. A final remark

One thing I learned in my journey is that we cannot stop the soul-touching research once it starts. Regardless of its costliness, whether to our health or savings, the pursuit is soul-sustaining and worthwhile, and sometimes its results through serendipity moments are also fruitful and "sweet". Through my own experiences, I hope to facilitate the understanding of how the "soul factor" might contribute to the greatness of serendipity moments.

Conducting research is like having a conversation with the world, trying to make sense of the world to ourselves and others. For the sake of the conversation, a researcher must develop an ability to feel one's soul resonated so deeply with something, which means to be exposed and challenged. I would like to end this chapter with a note on vulnerability by the English poet David Whyte (Popova, 2020):

> "To run from vulnerability is to run from the essence of our nature; the attempt to be invulnerable is the vain attempt to become something we are not and most especially, to close off our understanding of the grief of others. More seriously, in refusing our vulnerability, we refuse the help needed at every turn of our existence and immobilize the essential, tidal, and conversational foundations of our identity."

Chapter references

La, V.-P., & Vuong, Q.-H. (2019). bayesvl: Visually learning the graphical structure of Bayesian networks and performing MCMC with 'Stan'. *The Comprehensive R Archive Network (CRAN)*.

Popova, M. (2020). *David Whyte on vulnerability, presence, and how we enlarge ourselves by surrendering to the uncontrollable.* Brainpickings. Retrieved from (January 03, 2022) https://www.brainpickings.org/2016/04/11/david-whyte-vulnerability/

Robinson, A. (2020). The archaeology of Armageddon. *Nature, 578*(7796), 510-512.

Vuong, Q.-H., Bui, Q.-K., La, V.-P., Vuong, T.-T., Ho, M.-T., Nguyen, H.-K. T., ... Ho, M.-T. (2019). Cultural evolution in Vietnam's early 20th century: a Bayesian networks analysis of Hanoi Franco-Chinese house designs. *Social Sciences & Humanities Open, 1*(1), 100001.

Vuong, Q.-H., Bui, Q.-K., La, V.-P., Vuong, T.-T., Nguyen, V.-H. T., Ho, M.-T., ... Ho, M.-T. (2018). Cultural additivity: behavioural insights from the interaction of Confucianism, Buddhism and Taoism in folktales. *Palgrave Communications, 4,* 143.

Vuong, Q.-H., La, V.-P., Nguyen, M.-H., Ho, M.-T., Tran, T., & Ho, M.-T. (2020). Bayesian analysis for social data: a step-by-step protocol and interpretation. *MethodsX, 7,* 100924.

Vuong, Q.-H., Le, T.-T., La, V.-P., Nguyen, T. T. H., Ho, M.-T., Khuc, Q., & Nguyen, M.-H. (2022). Covid-19 vaccines production and societal immunization under the serendipity-mindsponge-3D knowledge management theory and conceptual framework. *Humanities and Social Sciences Communications, 9,* 22.

Vuong, Q. H. (2015). Be rich or don't be sick: estimating Vietnamese patients' risk of falling into destitution. *SpringerPlus, 4*(1), 529.

Kingfisher

©2017 Bui Quang Khiem

Chapter 9:
Revisiting the floppy-eared-rabbit serendipity circumstance

Minh-Hoang Nguyen, Viet-Phuong La, Tam-Tri Le, Quy Khuc

❧ • ☙

To validate the new theory of serendipity that we have presented, the case of "floppy-eared-rabbit" with Dr. Lewis Thomas and Dr. Aaron Kellner was used as an example. We go through each important stage in the story and explain the events in terms of serendipity's conditionality, survival motives, and information process. The characteristics of serendipity gain and loss phenomena are also interpreted in a similar manner.

❧ • ☙

9.1. Introduction

The floppy-eared-rabbit serendipity case reported by Barber and Fox (1958) is a famous and typical example of serendipity gained and serendipity lost in scientific and medicinal discoveries. The two eminent medical researchers – Dr. Lewis Thomas from New York University and Dr. Aaron Kellner from Cornell University – noticed the unusual anomaly that rabbits' ears "flopped" when the creatures received injections of the enzyme papain. Both were conducting research in experimental pathology, affiliated with distinguished medical schools, and seemingly had the same level of research ability. However, although both Dr. Thomas's and Dr. Kellner's attention were caught by the "bizarre" and entertaining qualities of the papain's

https://doi.org/10.2478/9788366675865-015

effect on rabbits' ears, Dr. Thomas successfully capitalized on the unexpected phenomenon, whereas Dr. Kellner did not. Given these features, the floppy-eared-rabbit circumstance is highly suitable for observing the serendipity process from both perspectives: a person successfully achieving serendipity outcomes and a person missing the chance to achieve the outcomes.

For validating our proposed theory of serendipity (see Chapter 6) and conditions to improve the success probability of serendipity (see Chapter 7), we aim to apply them to reinterpret the process leading to serendipity in the floppy-eared-rabbit circumstance. In the next section, we analyze the responses of Dr. Thomas and Dr. Kellner about their experience with the floppy-eared-rabbit phenomenon. The analysis's materials are retrieved from the interviews of Barber and Fox (1958) with both Dr. Thomas and Dr. Kellner. Finally, we discuss the main points inducted from the analysis on the reexamination.

9.2. The floppy-eared-rabbit serendipity

According to the interview responses of Dr. Thomas and Dr. Kellner, Dr. Thomas had two times of catching unexpected information, while Dr. Kellner only had one. Two researchers' first observation of unexpected the floppy-eared-rabbit phenomenon quite at the same time.

- **The first unexpected moment**

The first time Dr. Thomas saw the phenomenon could be traced back to the accidental use of papain for his investigation on the relationship between cardiac and blood vessel lesions and proteolytic enzymes, which was a clear expression of his social survival demand. In his interview response to Barber and Fox (1958), he said that:

Thomas: " I was trying to explore the notion that the cardiac and blood vessel lesions in certain hypersensitivity states may be due to release of proteolytic enzymes. It's an attractive idea on which there's little evidence. And it's been picked up at some time or another by almost everyone working on hypersensitivity. For this investigation, I used trypsin because it was the most available enzyme around the laboratory, and I got nothing. We also happened to have papain; I don't know where it had come from; but because it was there, I tried it."

Through his words, it can be seen that Dr. Thomas was in need of materials to pursue his then research but had limited resources for the intended investigation. We are not completely sure about Thomas's true motives to conduct and pursue his research at that time. However, it was highly likely that the desire to sustain and develop his career or scientific work was his main motivation. In that case, it is a form of social survival demand. This survival demand emerged when the environment was somewhat resource-limited (here, Dr. Thomas has three enzymes available for testing in his lab, including papain – which he did not know where it had come from). Without this seemingly subtle survival motive, Dr. Thomas could probably not have decided to try using papain on rabbits, and it could not have led to any discovery afterward.

Dr. Kellner used papain on rabbits at about the same time as Dr. Thomas (around 1951). His use of papain was intentional, but the unexpectedness only came when he actually noticed the strange reaction in rabbits' ears.

> **Kellner:** "we called them the floppy-eared rabbits [...]. Five or six years ago, we published our first article on the work we were doing with papain; that was in 1951, and our definitive article was published in 1954 [...]. We gave papain to the animals and we had done it thirty or forty times before we noticed these changes in the rabbits' ears."

After noticing the striking uniformity of rabbits' ears after injection of the enzyme papain, Dr. Kellner also did what Dr. Thomas did: investigate the causes behind the phenomenon. By doing this, Dr. Kellner might also expect that his discovery of the factors leading to the floppy-eared-rabbits phenomenon might give him competitive advantages in his career, which was a type of social survival.

However, several conditions in the mindset and environment must be satisfied to successfully capitalize on the unexpected information (an event or phenomenon) and translate it into a competitive (or strategic) advantage. These conditions include personal backgrounds (e.g., knowledge, skills, insights), resources (e.g., time, money), and emotional factors (e.g., curiosity, happiness). In the case of Dr. Thomas, he had a very strong desire to seek an answer for satisfying his curiosity because he saw a large potent in the uniformity of rabbits' ears after papain injections.

> **Thomas:** "It was one of the most uniform reactions I'd ever seen in biology. It always happened. And it looked as if something important must have happened to cause this reaction."

Nevertheless, at the time, Dr. Thomas lacked the sufficient ability to find a proper explanation for the floppy-eared phenomena in rabbits.

In other words, his expertise within the discipline and out of discipline was not sufficient to capitalize on the unexpected information.

In particular, his wrong preconceptions, expectations, and convictions prevented him from finding out the correct answer:

> **Thomas:** "I chased it like crazy. But I didn't do the right thing [...]. I did the expected things. I had sections cut, and I had them stained by all the techniques available at the time. And I studied what I believed to be the constituents of a rabbit's ear. I looked at all the sections, but I couldn't see anything the matter [...]. I hadn't thought of cartilage. You're not likely to, because it's not considered interesting [...]. I know my own idea has always been that cartilage is a quiet, inactive tissue."

Moreover, the limited time and rabbits also refrained Dr. Thomas from continuing his investigation.

> **Thomas:** "(Thomas was) terribly busy working on another problem at the time. [...] I had already used all the rabbits I could afford. So I was able to persuade myself to abandon this other research."

In the case of Dr. Kellner, besides the misleading of his preconceptions about cartilage and lack of time, Dr. Kellner's curiosity on the phenomenon was also not high enough to carry out a disciplined investigation process into the matter, so he and his associates determined to close out their interest in the floppy-eared-rabbit phenomenon.

> **Kellner:** "I was a little curious about it at the time, and followed it up to the extent of making sections of the rabbits' ears. [...] Every laboratory technician we've

had since 1951 has known about these floppy ears because we've used them to assay papain, to tell us if it's potent and how potent. […] we knew all about it, and used it that way … as a rule of thumb.[…] (Kellner had never had) any intention of publishing it as a method of assaying papain."

Two other reasons prevented Dr. Kellner from continuing to investigate the phenomenon. He had already had a direction or established research interest to follow at the time, so his motivation to pursue the floppy-eared-rabbit research was not high. Moreover, he and his associates might find that they had gained enough benefits from the unexpected phenomenon by using it as an assay test for the potency and amount of papain to be injected. He told Barber and Fox (1958) that:

> **Kellner:** "Every laboratory technician we've had since 1951 has known about these floppy ears because we've used them to assay papain, to tell us if it's potent and how potent […]. If the rabbit lived and his ears drooped, it was just right […]. We knew all about it, and used it that way […] as a rule of thumb."

- **The second unexpected moment**

Despite the failure in the first attempt, Dr. Thomas's curiosity kept the desire to know the causes behind the floppy-eared-rabbit in his mind. Though not directly, Thomas still consistently turned on his "radar" and sought information related to the phenomenon. This is why when Barber and Fox (1958) told Dr. Thomas that they knew about another medical scientist who had also noticed the reversible collapse of rabbits' ears, Dr. Thomas had already known that scientist was Kellner.

> **Thomas:** "That must be Kellner. He must have seen it.
> He was doomed to see it."

Dr. Thomas also read two other reports of Dr. Kellner about the effects of papain injection on rabbits, namely: "Selective necrosis of cardiac and skeletal muscle induced experimentally by means of proteolytic enzyme solutions given intravenously" (Kellner & Robertson, 1954) and "Blood Coagulation Defect Induced in Rabbits by Papain Solutions Injected Intravenously" (Kellner et al., 1951). Dr. Thomas's demand for more information related to the floppy-eared-rabbit phenomenon was also indicated through his behaviors. He shared it with other colleagues from pathology, biochemistry, and clinical investigation for out-of-discipline knowledge. Sometimes, he had to redo the experiment to persuade his skeptical colleagues about the phenomenon. Furthermore, he performed the experiment again in his class. The "bizarre" phenomenon occurred again when performing other experiments and immediately recalled him of the floppy-eared rabbit. Consciously or unconsciously, his intention to seek information related to the phenomenon persisted, even after he stopped it temporarily.

His underlying survival motive still had a huge contribution in the second unexpected moment. What encouraged him to continue pursuing the research again was a breakthrough when he taught and performed the experiment to "convey to students what experimental pathology is like." The desire to convey his knowledge and ideology to his students – a type of social survival demand – led him to change his method of examining rabbit tissues (comparing the ear tissue of rabbits injected with papain and that of rabbits not receiving papain), and eventually discover the drastic change occurring in the cartilaginous tissue. Apart from the accidental discovery in the seminar class with medical students, the motivation to find a new potential research direction when other studies reached an impasse – another type of social survival demand – also contributed to his determination to seek the answer for the floppy-eared rabbit phenomenon again. At the time, he had enough interest and resources (money and time) to pursue the research.

9.3. Discussion

Former studies have presented several approaches for explaining serendipity phenomena (André et al., 2009; Copeland, 2019; Cunha, 2005; Cunha et al., 2010; De Rond, 2014; Lawley & Tompkins, 2011; Makri & Blandford, 2012; McCay-Peet & Toms, 2010; McCay-Peet & Toms, 2015; Mendonça et al., 2008; Merton & Barber, 2004; Rubin et al., 2011). On the approach of information processing (Levy et al., 2007; Napier & Vuong, 2013; Nguyen et al., 2021; Vuong et al., 2022; Vuong & Napier, 2015; Vuong, 2016; Vuong & Napier, 2014), here we go deeper into the mechanism of serendipity, aiming to have a more consistent framework for analyzing serendipity phenomena.

From the Barber and Fox's (1958) interviews with Dr. Thomas and Dr. Kellner, we could see that although Dr. Thomas and Dr. Kellner both observed the unexpected floppy-eared-rabbit event, Dr. Thomas successfully took advantage of the information and turned it into his competitive advantage (Vuong, 2018), while Dr. Kellner did not. The contrasting serendipity gained and lost results could be explained by the new serendipity theory proposed in Chapter 6 and five conditions to improve the serendipity success chance described in Chapter 7.

The first condition is the availability of information. If Dr. Kellner did not have the knowledge about papain, he must not have used it for the experiment and observed the information about the floppiness of rabbits' ears. If there was no papain in the laboratory at the time of the experiment, Dr. Thomas must not have been aware of the enzyme and tried using it on the rabbits.

The second condition is the correct direction. Both Dr. Thomas and Dr. Kellner proactively pursued research to find the causes behind the phenomenon, which was the right direction to create something valuable (Vuong, 2019). Such decisions were driven by their demands for social survival (e.g., competitiveness in career). Although Dr. Thomas and Dr. Kellner's decisions to study the floppy-eared-rabbit phenomenon were right, they did not succeed in understanding the causes behind it. It was because they lacked within- and out-of-discipline expertise (inappropriate preconceptions, expectations, and convictions about cartilage) and disciplined process (due to insufficient time and resources).

Due to his established interest, Dr. Kellner determined to pursue another direction. The new direction led him to close out the desire to know more about the phenomenon of reversible collapse of rabbits' ears after injecting papain intravenously and employ it as an assay test for the potency and amount of papain to be injected. Following the new direction, Dr. Kellner also successfully published two other works based on serendipitous results occurring when injecting papain intravenously to rabbits (Kellner and Robertson, 1954; Kellner et al., 1951).

Meanwhile, Dr. Thomas still remained interested in the floppiness in rabbits' ears and sought information related to the phenomenon, though not active like before. Absorbing out-of-discipline information (from colleagues in pathology, biochemistry, and clinical investigation) and experimenting multiple times might lead Dr. Thomas to the second unexpected moment when he was giving a lecture to his medical students. He determined to pursue the experiment again actively and finally successfully capitalized on the unexpected information found priorly (Thomas, 1956). This time, the driving force of social survival demand was clear as Dr. Thomas was facing impasses in his other experiments and found the investigation into floppy-eared-rabbit event a potential direction to progress (possibly, for meeting career demands or improving competitive advantage).

In general, this floppy-eared-rabbit story is an exemplary case that validates the proposed theory in Chapter 6, which states: "serendipity is an ability to notice, evaluate, and take advantage of unexpected information for survival (both natural and social), of which its outcome and success rate are conditional on the individual mindset and environment". Such conditions can be summarized as the availability of information, appropriate direction, disciplined process, sufficient openness and good observation skills, and sufficient experience, knowledge, expertise, and wisdom.

From a personal perspective of authors, we also reflect and realize such serendipity-related conditions in the research processes of some of our major studies (Nguyen et al., 2021; Vuong, 2020; Vuong et al., 2018; Vuong et al., 2020; Vuong et al., 2021a, 2021b).

Chapter references

André, P., Schraefel, M., Teevan, J., & Dumais, S. T. (2009). Discovery is never by chance: designing for (un) serendipity. *Proceedings of the seventh ACM conference on Creativity and cognition*, 305-314.

Barber, B., & Fox, R. C. (1958). The case of the floppy-eared rabbits: An instance of serendipity gained and serendipity lost. *American Journal of Sociology, 64*(2), 128-136.

Copeland, S. (2019). On serendipity in science: discovery at the intersection of chance and wisdom. *Synthese, 196*(6), 2385-2406.

Cunha, M. P. (2005). Serendipity: Why some organizations are luckier than others. *FEUNL Working Paper Series*, 472.

Cunha, M. P. E., Clegg, S. R., & Mendonça, S. (2010). On serendipity and organizing. *European Management Journal, 28*(5), 319-330.

De Rond, M. (2014). The structure of serendipity. *Culture and Organization, 20*(5), 342-358.

Kellner, A., & Robertson, T. (1954). Selective necrosis of cardiac and skeletal muscle induced experimentally by means of proteolytic enzyme solutions given intravenously. *The Journal of Experimental Medicine, 99*(4), 387-404.

Kellner, A., Robertson, T., & Mott, H. (1951). Blood coagulation defect induced in rabbits by papain solutions injected intravenously. *Federation Proceedings, 10*(1).

Lawley, J., & Tompkins, P. (2011). *Maximising serendipity: the art of recognising and fostering unexpected potential - A systemic approach to change*. The Clean Collection. Retrieved from (December 31, 2021) https://cleanlanguage.co.uk/articles/articles/224/1/Maximising-Serendipity/Page1.html

Levy, O., Beechler, S., Taylor, S., & Boyacigiller, N. A. (2007). What we talk about when we talk about 'global mindset': managerial cognition in multinational corporations. *Journal of International Business Studies, 38*(2), 231-258.

Makri, S., & Blandford, A. (2012). Coming across information serendipitously–Part 1: a process model. *Journal of Documentation, 68*(5), 684-705.

McCay-Peet, L., & Toms, E. G. (2010). The process of serendipity in knowledge work. Proceedings of the Third Symposium on Information Interaction in Context,

McCay-Peet, L., & Toms, E. G. (2015). Investigating serendipity: how it unfolds and what may influence it. *Journal of the Association for Information Science and Technology, 66*(7), 1463-1476.

Mendonça, S., Cunha, M., & Clegg, S. R. (2008). Unsought innovation: serendipity in organizations. Entrepreneurship and Innovation—Organizations, Institutions, Systems and Regions Conference, Copenhagen.

Merton, R. K., & Barber, E. (2004). *The travels and adventures of serendipity: a study in sociological semantics and the sociology of science.* Princeton University Press.

Napier, N., & Vuong, Q. H. (2013). Serendipity as a strategic advantage? In T. Wilkinson (Ed.), *Strategic management in the 21st century* (pp. 175-199). Praeger/ABC-Clio.

Nguyen, M.-H., Le, T.-T., Nguyen, H.-K. T., Ho, M.-T., Nguyen, H. T. T., & Vuong, Q.-H. (2021). Alice in Suicideland: exploring the suicidal ideation mechanism through the sense of connectedness and help-seeking behaviors. *International Journal of Environmental Research and Public Health, 18*(7), 3681.

Rubin, V. L., Burkell, J., & Quan-Haase, A. (2011). Facets of serendipity in everyday chance encounters: a grounded theory approach to blog analysis. *Information Research, 16*(3), 488.

Thomas, L. (1956). Reversible collapse of rabbit ears after intravenous papain, and prevention of recovery by cortisone. *The Journal of Experimental Medicine, 104*(2), 245.

Vuong, Q. H. (2016). Global mindset as the integration of emerging socio-cultural values through mindsponge processes: A transition economy perspective. In J. Kuada (Ed.), *Global mindsets: exploration and perspectives* (pp. 109-126). Routledge.

Vuong, Q.-H. (2018). The (ir)rational consideration of the cost of science in transition economies. *Nature Human Behaviour, 2,* 5.

Vuong, Q.-H. (2019). Breaking barriers in publishing demands a proactive attitude. *Nature Human Behaviour, 3*(10), 1034-1034.

Vuong, Q.-H. (2020). Reform retractions to make them more transparent. *Nature, 582,* 149.

Vuong, Q.-H., et al. (2018). Cultural additivity: behavioural insights from the interaction of Confucianism, Buddhism and Taoism in folktales. *Palgrave Communications, 4,* 143.

Vuong, Q.-H., et al. (2020). On how religions could accidentally incite lies and violence: folktales as a cultural transmitter. *Palgrave Communications, 6,* 82.

Vuong, Q.-H., Le, T.-T., La, V.-P., Nguyen, T. T. H., Ho, M.-T., Khuc, Q., & Nguyen, M.-H. (2022). Covid-19 vaccines production and societal immunization under the serendipity-mindsponge-3D knowledge management theory and conceptual framework. *Humanities and Social Sciences Communications, 9,* 22.

Vuong, Q. H., & Napier, N. K. (2014). Making creativity: the value of multiple filters in the innovation process. *International Journal of Transitions and Innovation Systems, 3*(4), 294-327.

Vuong, Q.-H., & Napier, N. K. (2015). Acculturation and global mindsponge: an emerging market perspective. *International Journal of Intercultural Relations, 49,* 354-367.

Vuong, Q.-H., Nguyen, M.-H., & Le, T.-T. (2021a). Home scholarly culture, book selection reason, and academic performance: Pathways to book reading interest among secondary school students. *European Journal of Investigation in Health, Psychology and Education, 11*(2), 468-495.

Vuong, Q.-H., Nguyen, M.-H., & Le, T.-T. (2021b). *A mindsponge-based investigation into the psycho-religious mechanism behind suicide attacks*. De Gruyter / Sciendo.

Kingfisher

©2017 Bui Quang Khiem

Chapter 10:
Environments and cultures that nurture serendipity strikes

Quan-Hoang Vuong, Minh-Hoang Nguyen, Quy Khuc, Tam-Tri Le

❧ • ☙

Based on the properties and mechanism of serendipity presented in former chapters, this chapter discusses how to create an environment for higher serendipity encounters and attainment possibilities. We examine four types of environments with different navigational and useful information concentration combinations. Building a pro-serendipity culture will help create environments that value and supports serendipity across fields. Additionally, we also address the notion that serendipity is a skill. Thus, it can produce either good or bad impacts on a collective level, depending on the ultimate purposes behind it.

❧ • ☙

10.1. Environments' impacts on serendipity encounter and attainment

There are two main types of information in a problem-solving process – navigational and useful – in the environment (sources of information), which determines its effectiveness and efficiency. The environment here should be understood as the total of all external information sources, including sensory stimuli from observable phenomena and social information exchanges. Regarding serendipity,

https://doi.org/10.2478/9788366675865-016

we aim to describe environments that increase our chance of encountering and capitalizing "unexpected information" – special information pieces that may activate the serendipity phenomenon.

The navigational information helps set the right direction toward a goal, while useful information serves as the "building blocks" to construct the road toward that goal. The unexpected information can be of either type, and its values differ in every specific context for every specific individual. Thus, to increase the chance of finding the right missing piece related to one's particular situation, the environment should provide a high chance of getting both types of information. In other words, we do not know in advance what values of the missing piece coming from the serendipity strike would be; so, the wise move is to try to get as much of the potential ones as possible. Here, it is important to note that the act of finding the missing piece itself also requires a good direction and the right resources (e.g., the right question and suitable expertise).

The density of navigational and useful information can be low or high in specific contexts. The combinations of their degrees of concentration can be categorized into four distinct environments, as presented in Figure 9.1.

- Environment A: Information of both types is scarce. One is likely to progress slowly in this environment and head towards inappropriate directions.
- Environment B: Useful information is abundant but navigational information is scarce. One is likely to progress rapidly in this environment but faces a high risk of heading towards inappropriate directions.
- Environment C: Navigational information is abundant but useful information is scarce. One is likely to head towards

appropriate directions, but their progress speed is slow in this environment.

- Environment D: Information of both types are abundant. One is likely to progress rapidly and head to appropriate directions in this environment.

In environment A, it is very challenging to know where one should progress towards and how to get there. Without proper navigation and constructive values, a person or organization in this type of environment will, unfortunately, depend heavily on pure luck for innovation, which certainly is not a reliable strategy. In environment B, despite having sufficient useful information (e.g., knowledge, social connections), the lack of navigational information will likely lead to poor decisions on the direction of action. This can potentially waste substantial resources due to the low effectiveness resulting from putting efforts into solving the wrong problems. It should be noted that the act of navigating will set the scope of scanning for the respective information, so a wrong direction will likely lead one to ignore or reject information that is otherwise a potential serendipity moment.

In environment C, while having a good vision, the lack of necessary constructive information will cause the progress to the goal to be very slow due to the low efficiency of operation. In survival contexts (whether natural or social), time is a crucial factor and a slow competitor is likely a "weak" competitor. For example, think of a company that guesses precisely where to look for the potential missing piece which could be used to innovate a particular product. Still, the lack of expertise takes them ten years to successfully innovate the product, and the market has long shifted away from that kind of merchandise. Therefore, considering all the other combinations with higher chances of failure, environment D is optimal in assisting individuals or organizations to reach their potential serendipity moments more easily.

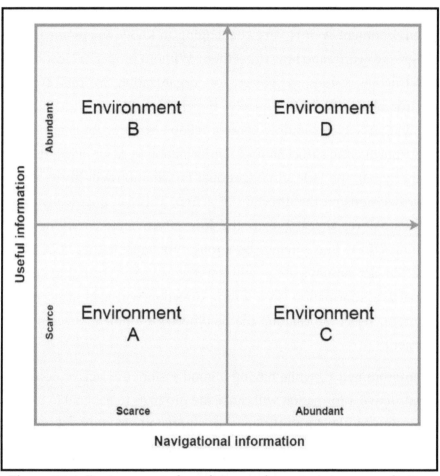

Figure 10.1: Environments benefiting and constraining serendipity

10.2. Building a pro-serendipity culture

From both the scenarios presented in chapter 7 and the discussion on information environments above, we can see the importance of both the acts of "navigating" and "moving/constructing". In a "linear operation", we may expect to set the direction first and then "move" toward the target information. However, even in a simple process where the target "stays in the same position", the initial direction is unlikely to be accurate, especially over "long-distance" (in more complex problems). Thus, it is necessary to re-estimate the direction regularly (imagine if a captain only looks at the compass once on the first day of a 1000-day voyage). This issue is even more important when we consider real-world situations where the "position" of the targeted information keeps changing due to complex interactions within a dynamic system.

For example, we might guess that the missing information has a good chance to be found by observing a certain event; then we start to make preparation to get to that specific event; by the time we reach the estimated destination, the event has changed properties (in terms of values, the target information has "moved away"). To visualize a simplified case, imagine a captain trying to go toward an unanchored buoy; if the captain does not adjust the direction regularly, the ship will likely miss the buoy carried away by ocean currents.

Navigation is crucial because spending efforts in the wrong direction is costly on many levels, but planning too much without making enough efforts to search for the target will hinder success. As energy, time, and other resources for a project/problem are limited, there is a possible dilemma about how much to spend on each type of action (navigating or moving). We can think of the image of the meerkats – a species of small mammals (about half to one kilogram) living in the arid regions of South Africa; these animals are quite famous for the iconic image of them standing up still and tall to survey their surroundings. These little animals can reach a top speed of approximately nine meters per second when running. Similarly, in a certain project, we need to temporarily stop sometimes and turn on our "radar" to scan for targets and set/confirm our direction. We need to intensely focus on completing actual tasks to move closer toward those scanned targets. Balancing these two types of action is the art of increasing the possibility of finding invaluable information deep within the unknown. To some degree, we can see similarities in how a meerkat tries to find its tasty food across the vast savanna. Again, it is worth emphasizing that both the "what" question (navigation) and "how" question (operation) are built upon one's background knowledge and mindset under heavy influences of culture (Vuong & Napier, 2015; Vuong, 2016; Vuong & Napier, 2014; Huynh, 2020).

An environment with its holding information plays a crucial role in the serendipity process (Mendonça, Cunha, et al., 2008). Here we focus on the collective and organizational levels. In reality, each information type's content (values) is heavily context-based, perceived differently in each field, organization, and group of people. Thus, building a pro-serendipity culture will help create environments with a high concentration of navigational and useful information.

Four important elements in building a collective and organizational culture facilitating innovation and serendipity are briefly presented here. Firstly, conditions for information exchange (especially out-of-discipline information) should be provided by supporting the formation of social networks to keep a "free flow of information" (Cunha et al., 2010). Secondly, it should be a culture that supports being open and willing to share a wide range of ideas on the basis of trust (Cunha et al., 2010; Mendonça, Cunha, et al., 2008; Nguyen et al., 2021; Vuong et al., 2021b). Thirdly, the culture should have a certain degree of tolerance toward experiments (Dew, 2009), where inefficiency, dissent, and failure may be the environment for formulating new ideas and perspectives. Fourthly, collectives and organizations need to integrate the value of serendipity into their mindsets, understanding the role of serendipity in relation to their purposes and accepting what it takes to promote serendipity (e.g., in allocating resources, hiring experts, and creating a working environment). It is also worth noting that the success resulting from serendipity will provide positive feedback and may justify the costs and efforts to create and maintain a pro-serendipity environment (Vuong, 2018).

Regarding the purpose of increasing serendipity possibility, while collectives and organizations often focus on providing useful information for members, navigational information may sometimes be neglected. For every collective and organization, the values of navigational information can be of various levels and directions, and most importantly, largely context-based. On the most integral level, this information is strongly related to the purpose of the main functions and activities of the group. For example, car producers aim to increase car sales, and climate scientists aim at innovations that effectively combat climate problems. This level of navigational information has a strong connection with survival desires. Other forms of navigational information may include methods to find potentially good information sources (e.g., providing social networks) or general wisdom about conducting work as well as personal life (e.g., reading habits, being proactive toward opportunities or crisis). Normally, people in positions of seniors or executives should be responsible for providing navigational information to other organization members.

Scientific research is a profession requiring a high degree of innovation, and serendipity is widely considered tremendously valuable. The work of doing science itself can be considered a culture

(Pickering, 1992). We can see the role of such culture in the story of Ernest Solvay below of how he benefited from serendipity and was also a person who greatly contributed to building environments and culture for facilitating innovation in science. Many top scientists in physics and chemistry attended the Solvay Conferences were or later became Nobel laureates. They followed a disciplined system of scientific conduct, which was established and well maintained over generations of scientists. In turn, scientists of the current generation try to keep, improve, and pass down those hard-earned cultural values as preparation for the future.

A good scientific culture is built upon brilliant minds, systematic plans, and great efforts (Vuong, 2019), reasonably justified for its seemingly high costs in the public's eyes (Vuong, 2018). Considering the importance of building and maintaining a good culture of science, besides conducting good research projects, ensuring high educational quality for the next generations is also very important (Anderson et al., 2011; Pham & Ho, 2020). One of the popular practices to prepare good conditions for serendipity is reading. A good reading culture will enhance people's knowledge (useful information) and their directions (navigational information) toward seeking the right knowledge for solving the right problems. Building high-quality educational cultures (e.g., reading culture) requires cooperation from various sides: children (e.g., self-efficacy, proactiveness), parents (e.g., home scholarly culture), teachers, school environment, and society (Hart, 2013; Miller, 2010; Uzzell, 1999; Van Kleeck et al., 2003; Vuong, 2019; Vuong et al., 2021a).

We can see that a pro-serendipity environment is built with multiple layers of social activities and must be kept over time and human generations. Sometimes, the initiation leading to building a better environment for more future innovations is itself a moment of serendipity. In the story from former chapters of this book, we have also looked at the story of Dr. Vuong's new theory on building an eco-surplus culture (Vuong, 2021a, 2021b), starting from his bird-related serendipity moments. Next, it is worth looking at how the discovery (through serendipity) of the ammonia-soda process allowed Ernest Solvay to have the necessary conditions for contributing to the improvement of the global scientific culture.

10.3. Ernest Solvay: In the building of pro-serendipity cultures

The reflection on Ernest Solvay's life and work greatly influenced how Dr. Quan-Hoang Vuong developed his thoughts about the utmost importance of building a good culture of science and how it can lead scientists to wondrous innovations (Bach & Vuong, 2015). In 1933, ten years after Solvay's passing, when his statue was unveiled at Avenue Franklin Roosevelt (Brussels) in the presence of the King of the Belgians and the Duke of Brabant, the journal *Nature* published a short piece named "Monument to Ernest Solvay", in which the following sentences were stated at the end: "Mr. Runciman, President of the Board of Trade, in a speech delivered on October 20, when dealing with the question of trade recovery, said that 'one first-class invention is worth fifty Acts of Parliament'. To that class of invention Solvay's belongs." ("Monument to Ernest Solvay," 1932).

Ernest Gaston Joseph Solvay (1838-1922) was a Belgian chemist and industrialist. In 1861, the major serendipity moment came when he obtained sodium carbonate (soda ash - Na_2CO_3) after mixing table salt with ammonia and carbonic acid gas in his experimentation room. This later led to the well-known "Solvay process" of producing soda ash from inexpensive and widely available resources of brine (source of sodium chloride – NaCl) and limestone (source of calcium carbonate - $CaCO_3$) with recyclable ammonia (NH_3) as the "catalyst". Solvay was unaware that other chemists had described the reaction. Industrial applications had been attempted to certain degrees, which turned out to be a good thing as he established his company in 1863. The company had a rocky start (even came close to bankruptcy). However, Solvay stuck to his vision and began large-scale production in 1865 while continuing to improve the technical aspect of the process. Solvay reaped immense success in 1870-1880 and expanded production to an international scale. In 1900, 95% of soda ash consumed worldwide was produced using the Solvay process. In 2020, the company had a net sales of €8.9 billion. Looking back, we can see that the chemical discovery in 1861 became a crucial serendipity moment in relation to the huge success of Solvay. Still, this relative value emerged conditionally due to his particular mindset and direction of actions. Otherwise, the discovery would simply stay at the level of chemistry curiosity and would not turn into the impactful industrial innovation we witness through history.

Suppose we wonder what conditions made Ernest Solvay become the person he was; we should also look at the efforts he put in trying to create such conditions for other generations of innovators. Solvay was not just a talented scientist and a brilliant entrepreneur. He was also a great philanthropist who significantly contributed to improving the global science culture using financial power from his business. In 1902, he founded the Solvay Institute of Sociology (*Institut de Sociologie Solvay*) and, in 1903, the Solvay Business school (*École de Commerce Solvay*). In 1911, the first Solvay Conference (*Conseil Solvay*) on "Radiation and the Quanta" was held, chaired by Hendrik Lorentz and attended by the world's most important brains such as Albert Einstein, Marie Curie, Ernest Rutherford, Henri Poincaré, and Max Planck.

From this first success, Solvay founded the International Solvay Institute for Physics in 1912 and the International Solvay Institute for Chemistry in 1913; the two later merged into the International Solvay Institutes for Physics and Chemistry, which has been organizing the Solvay Conference once every two years up to the present day. The fifth Solvay Conference on Physics held in 1927 on "Electrons and Photons" was an important milestone for quantum theory research, with notable names among participants such as Niels Bohr, Werner Heisenberg, Erwin Schrödinger, and Paul Dirac. Solvay Conferences have largely been considered the most famous conferences in physics and chemistry, where great minds of the world meet and discuss current major problems, leading to the innovation of immense values to the advancement of humanity during the last century.

Besides supporting science, Ernest Solvay was also a pioneer in welfare policies such as pension (since 1878), 8-hour work time (since 1897), and paid leave (since 1913). Following the founder's vision, today, the Solvay multinational corporate also has more than two thousand researchers working in Research and Innovation Centers across many countries, expanding into new frontiers of the modern age such as green technologies.

We can see from the story of Ernest Solvay that to reach the peak of innovation – theoretical advancements and practical progress – requires a great deal of personal efforts, holistic sociocultural background development, and a philosophical core that pursues true virtue and aesthetics. Again, the combination of a good direction and a well-disciplined operation is proved to be necessary for detecting and utilizing precious information for solving the big questions of humanity (Vuong et al., 2022).

Knowing this, we come to appreciate even more the current "ecosystem" of science, which has been built on the shoulders of giants from the very early age of humankind, consistently up to this very moment. The culture is the "hatchery" of serendipity moments that shape the future of both science and society. The conditions for miracles are very difficult to create, but we know it is indeed worth the endeavors, looking at the history of innovation. Better technologies would someday replace Ernest Solvay's ammonia-soda process that dominated the industry – it is just the way of progress. However, his virtue and contributions to science and society will remain for many generations to come.

10.4. Serendipity: a neutral survival skill

People often talk about serendipity as a positive value, even as "miracles". However, as we have discussed its nature and mechanism in this book, serendipity should be considered a skill. A skill does not hold ethical value, so that it can be good, neutral, or bad, depending on the situation and perspectives. The subjective perceptions of "good" or "bad" are different among distinct individuals, groups, or collectives. On the motives of natural or social survival, one can physically, financially, or psychologically harm others based on noticing some perceived helpful information (or the values from a serendipity phenomenon). Such impacts of serendipity (as a skill) may be beneficial for a person or a group but harmful for other people or the collective human society.

From a natural survival perspective, think of how the innovations in making and using tools helped *Homo sapiens* have a big military advantage in terms of weapons (Shea & Sisk, 2010). *Homo sapiens* also had another major advantage in terms of our ability to strategize and deceive (Von Clausewitz, 2008). It is still debatable whether war between human species was one of the major reasons leading to other human species' extinction, leaving *Homo sapiens* as the only survivors today. However, it is clear that war has been a big part of our own species' history. In the famous ancient book "The Art of War" by Chinese military strategist Sun Tzu, there are many suggestions that one should act flexibly based on observing the states and environments of the battlegrounds (Tzu, 2021). One of the famous quotes from the book is, "兵者，诡道也" [all warfare is based on deception]. In order to successfully deceive the enemies, one must be able to utilize tactics outside the common sphere of knowledge – in other words, effective deceptions need innovation.

Let us look at a typical example of wrong ways to benefit from serendipity. "The Wolf of Wall Street" (2013, starring Leonardo DiCaprio – a globally famous actor and one of the youngest Oscar nominees) is an Academy Award-nominated film based on the memoir with the same name by American stockbroker Jordan Belfort (Belfort, 2007). The film tells the story about Belfort's brokerage firm – Stratton Oakmont – and its "pump and dump" fraudulent tactics of inflating the price of cheap stocks with misinformation and selling them at high prices. Belfort realized a loophole in the financial system and capitalized on it for personal profit gain. In a sense, that particular serendipity moment was beneficial for Belfort and his group at the time, greatly increasing his economic and social power. However, that personally valuable realization led to acts of scamming, which negatively impacted many other people and the whole financial system.

In recent years, blockchain technologies, cryptocurrencies, and non-fungible tokens (NFTs) have become a focus of innovative applications in business. Many have noticed potential opportunities and values in the technologies on this new information, which led to the current boom of new trends such as NFT metaverse (Napoli, 2021) and NFT in video games (Birnbaum, 2022). However, serendipity applications in this field need to be treated with proper consideration. Besides the risk of new financial frauds and exploitations, we need to carefully assess the negative environmental impacts of blockchain technologies, such as through cryptocurrency mining and transaction (Jiang et al., 2021; Krause & Tolaymat, 2018). Again, it is very important to be aware that serendipity can be used to create innovations that are deemed beneficial or unethical on collective levels, just like other skills and tools.

Thus, building cultures or environments with sufficient navigational and useful information towards collectively valuable, meaningful, and soul-touching ideologies will help create value-surplus for the human society through serendipity strikes.

Chapter references

Anderson, W. A., Banerjee, U., Drennan, C. L., Elgin, S. C. R., Epstein, I. R., Handelsman, J., ... Warner, I. M. (2011). Changing the culture of science education at research universities. *Science, 331*(6014), 152-153.

Belfort, J. (2007). *The Wolf of Wall Street*. Bantam Books.

Birnbaum, J. (2022). *Why video game makers see huge potential in Blockchain—and why problems loom for their new NFTs*. Forbes. Retrieved from (January 11, 2022) https://www.forbes.com/sites/justinbirnbaum/2022/01/06/why-video-game-makers-see-huge-potential-in-blockchain-and-why-problems-loom-for-their-new-nfts/?sh=6abd10f043d7

Chiến, B. N., & Hoang, V. Q. (2015). *Bằng chứng cuộc sống: suy ngẫm về phát triển bền vững Việt Nam*. NXB Chính trị quốc gia, Hà Nội.

Cunha, M. P. e., Clegg, S. R., & Mendonça, S. (2010). On serendipity and organizing. *European Management Journal, 28*(5), 319-330.

Dew, N. (2009). Serendipity in entrepreneurship. *Organization Studies, 30*(7), 735-753.

Hart, R. A. (2013). *Children's participation: The theory and practice of involving young citizens in community development and environmental care*. Routledge.

Huynh, T. L. D. (2020). Does culture matter social distancing under the COVID-19 pandemic? *Safety Science, 130*, 104872.

Jiang, S., Li, Y., Lu, Q., Hong, Y., Guan, D., Xiong, Y., & Wang, S. (2021). Policy assessments for the carbon emission flows and sustainability of Bitcoin blockchain operation in China. *Nature Communications, 12*, 1938.

Krause, M. J., & Tolaymat, T. (2018). Quantification of energy and carbon costs for mining cryptocurrencies. *Nature Sustainability, 1*(11), 711-718.

Mendonça, S., Cunha, M., & Clegg, S. R. (2008). Unsought innovation: serendipity in organizations. Entrepreneurship and Innovation—Organizations, Institutions, Systems and Regions Conference, Copenhagen.

Miller, D. (2010). *The book whisperer: Awakening the Inner Reader in Every Child*. John Wiley & Sons.

Monument to Ernest Solvay. (1932). *Nature, 130*, 657.

Napoli, R. (2021). *The NFT metaverse: building a blockchain world*. Forbes. Retrieved from (accessed on: January 13, 2022) https://www.forbes.com/sites/forbestechcouncil/2021/12/27/the-nft-metaverse-building-a-blockchain-world/?sh=4c5bab5a531c

Nguyen, M.-H., Le, T.-T., Nguyen, H.-K. T., Ho, M.-T., Nguyen, H. T. T., & Vuong, Q.-H. (2021). Alice in Suicideland: exploring the suicidal ideation mechanism through the sense of connectedness and help-seeking behaviors. *International Journal of Environmental Research and Public Health, 18*(7), 3681.

Pham, H.-H., & Ho, T.-T.-H. (2020). Toward a 'new normal' with e-learning in Vietnamese higher education during the post-COVID-19 pandemic. *Higher Education Research & Development, 39*(7), 1327–1331.

Pickering, A. (1992). *Science as practice and culture* (A. Pickering, Ed.). University of Chicago Press.

Shea, J. J., & Sisk, M. L. (2010). Complex projectile technology and Homo sapiens dispersal into western Eurasia. *PaleoAnthropology, 2010,* 100-122.

Tzu, S. (2021). *The art of war.* Vintage.

Uzzell, D. (1999). Education for environmental action in the community: new roles and relationships. *Cambridge Journal of Education, 29*(3), 397-413.

Van Kleeck, A., Stahl, S. A., & Bauer, E. B. (2003). *On reading books to children: Parents and teachers.* Routledge.

Von Clausewitz, C. (2008). *On war.* Princeton University Press.

Vuong, Q. H. (2016). Global mindset as the integration of emerging socio-cultural values through mindsponge processes: A transition economy perspective. In J. Kuada (Ed.), *Global mindsets: exploration and perspectives* (pp. 109-126). Routledge.

Vuong, Q. H., & Napier, N. K. (2014). Making creativity: the value of multiple filters in the innovation process. *International Journal of Transitions and Innovation Systems, 3*(4), 294-327.

Vuong, Q.-H. (2018). The (ir)rational consideration of the cost of science in transition economies. *Nature Human Behaviour, 2,* 5.

Vuong, Q.-H. (2019). Breaking barriers in publishing demands a proactive attitude. *Nature Human Behaviour, 3*(10), 1034.

Vuong, Q.-H. (2021a). The semiconducting principle of monetary and environmental values exchange. *Economics and Business Letters, 10*(3), 284-290.

Vuong, Q.-H. (2021b). Western monopoly of climate science is creating an eco-deficit culture. *Economy, Land & Climate Insight.* https://elc-insight.org/western-monopoly-of-climate-science-is-creating-an-eco-deficit-culture/

Vuong, Q.-H., & Napier, N. K. (2015). Acculturation and global mindsponge: an emerging market perspective. *International Journal of Intercultural Relations, 49,* 354-367.

Vuong, Q.-H., Le, T.-T., La, V.-P., Nguyen, T. T. H., Ho, M.-T., Khuc, Q., & Nguyen, M.-H. (2022). Covid-19 vaccines production and societal immunization under the serendipity-mindsponge-3D knowledge management theory and conceptual framework. *Humanities and Social Sciences Communications, 9,* 22.

Vuong, Q.-H., Nguyen, M.-H., & Le, T.-T. (2021a). Home scholarly culture, book selection reason, and academic performance: Pathways to book reading interest among secondary school students. *European Journal of Investigation in Health, Psychology and Education, 11*(2), 468-495.

Vuong, Q.-H., Nguyen, M.-H., & Le, T.-T. (2021b). *A mindsponge-based investigation into the psycho-religious mechanism behind suicide attacks.* De Gruyter / Sciendo.

Kingfisher

©2017 Bui Quang Khiem

Chapter 11:
Preliminary explanations of serendipity based on non-linear information process

Tam-Tri Le, Viet-Phuong La, Quy Khuc, Minh-Hoang Nguyen

ॐ • ॐ

After employing the mindsponge mechanism and 3D information process of creativity to explain the serendipity process in previous chapters, we realize that it may be helpful to delve into the relations between serendipity and the formulation of new values and information connections through non-linear processes. Thus, this chapter summarizes some preliminary attempts to use non-linear information processes to explain serendipity. We also briefly mention the benefits of information exchange among members of social groups and explain this approach.

ॐ • ॐ

11.1. Serendipity as an outcome of a non-linear thinking process?

"How do I think?" is an age-old philosophical question as well as a major focus in modern neuroscience and psychology. In normal contexts, non-linear thinking is often superficially referred to as a general "style of thinking" that considers multiple directions of solutions and makes many connections among a variety of reference information (Willems, 2016; Langhe et al., 2017). While this loosely defined concept has been applied in business and education through

https://doi.org/10.2478/9788366675865-017

certain models or indexes, the conceptualization of the term is insufficient, let alone examining its cognitive mechanism.

Tracing (being aware of each step in) a thinking process may appear harder than formulating the thought itself. It does not have to be a relatively complex thought to see this; for example, try to trace back how you came to understand the meaning of this sentence step by step. The mind uses a different approach when "showing" the results of thoughts to itself (being aware) compared to when the thinking occurs. Humans can make quite accurate estimations in a very short time without going through detailed reasoning. There are examples in mundane social interactions, such as deciding when to tell what joke to which friend during a conversation for the optimal expected result. Many people may call this type of short-cut thinking "intuition" (another insufficiently conceptualized term).

Perhaps, serendipity – discussed in problem-solving contexts – can be viewed as a sign pointing at non-linear thinking mechanisms. The structure of serendipity shows a "jump" in terms of information processing, where consistent observations (tracing/ awareness) cannot be made continuously from the initial problem to the final solution due to a gap in-between. From the observer's perspective, the "jump" is not only applicable to the connections (lines) but also to the problems or solutions (endpoints) as well.

Recent studies in neuroscience show multidimensional processing in terms of neuronal structure and activity in the brain (Gothard, 2020; Stringer et al., 2019). Here, non-linear thinking should be viewed as simultaneous processing multiple values and converging into a visible result (thought) – with the same properties described in the multi-filtering process of the mindsponge framework (Vuong et al., 2021b; Vuong, 2016; Vuong & Napier, 2015). The properties of the observed results can be categorized based on the directionality (active/controlled or "automatic" thinking) of the process as well as the pre-perception toward the result (expected or unexpected). Whichever the case, arguably, non-linear thinking is not a "style of thinking" as portrayed in common understanding nor any extraordinary thinking mode, but rather a natural mechanism of information processing in the brain, regardless of the degree of nonlinearity deemed by the observer. Most probably, the conversion to easily observable linear expressions in tracing/observing thinking requires additional calculation power and thus makes it appear not easy.

From "If a tree falls in a forest and no one is around to hear it, does it make a sound?", we ask if an idea is formed in the brain but cannot be observed and recognized, does it make any impact? This reflects a core issue: we do not know how often we have missed great ideas created by our own minds (serendipity moments).

The brain works continuously even when a person does not actively think (giving directions to the process – thinking – or demands to the result – thoughts). Even when actively thinking, one cannot fully track one's *own* thinking process. The brain can be seen as an automatic thought-factory that constantly produces ideas and thoughts. When awareness arises, some thoughts are selected for further evaluation; others are discarded due to having no or low perceived values; this also follows the mindsponge mechanism of information filtering (Nguyen et al., 2021; Nguyen & Vuong, 2021). In a normal condition, many thoughts are discarded automatically throughout the day.

Many generated thoughts are automatically discarded due to the lack of awareness (observation). The loss itself is also not observed; thus, we do not even know what happened. Active thinking has a higher degree of thought observation (motivated by the desire for results).

However, this state does not last long (normally a minor proportion of total awake time). In conditions of lower attention (low intensity of observation), it is more likely to be hit or miss. Still, the exact influencing factors of hit probability are generally unclear (consider the case of Archimedes).

During observation, the initial impressions of thoughts probably determine the prioritization of recognition. Think of lightning, the flashier ones are more observable, while those between clouds are mostly hidden. Ideas distract each other. It is also worth noting that due to the lack of careful evaluation at this initial point of observation, the less impressive idea may actually be more valuable and vice versa. This bias can be countered with a well-designed and objective system such as scientific recording.

Thinking and observing thoughts (being aware of thoughts) are two different types of mental processes. They happen in chronological order – thinking must finish (already produced a thought) before said thought can be observed (be known by oneself). Here, perhaps, the process of thinking (to be clear, not its result – thought) cannot be directly observed because it does not hold information values (unlike thoughts). Therefore, the awareness of thinking is indirect (through other thoughts about the effects of the thinking process). Additionally, to further explore the relationship between thought and thought awareness, consider the dream state - where the brain constructs all components, including the dream world, characters, and interactions, while the awareness is normally limited to a single perspective.

Upon complex problems, thinking can occur with high nonlinearity (simultaneous processing). Ideas formed during this time are highly abstract and new, thus are less comparable to stored reference information. This is particularly important when considering humans' heavy reliance on sensory perceptions (making connections to tangible entities) and languages (serve as anchors for abstract concepts). Therefore, it is even harder to realize the value of such ideas. Here we also argue that while thinking varies in the degree of nonlinearity, thought observation requires a linear operation (or it would not make sense). This can be the key to exploring the issues of low awareness toward one's own thoughts in the context of creating the optimal conditions for capturing serendipity moments (Vuong & Napier, 2014).

11.2. Serendipity classification using non-linear information process

Based on the thinking in the previous section, we aim to present some preliminary explanations of serendipity's typology using the nonlinear information process in this section. Specifically, we will explore the information process of each type of serendipity using a simplified approach of non-linear thinking based on the mindsponge framework (Vuong et al., 2021b; Vuong & Napier, 2015).

The serendipity types discussed here are based on the categorization presented in the works of Napier and Vuong (2013) and De Rond (2014). Such categorization is briefly presented as follows.

- Normal problem solving: Want to solve something, and the solution is an expected logical result.
- Type I serendipity: Want to solve something, but the solution comes from an unexpected source.
- Type II serendipity: Want to solve something but accidentally solve another problem instead.
- Type III serendipity: Formerly acquired information leads to an unexpected solution when the problem arises.

To begin with, we present some premises about simplified thinking processes.

- During a period of time, one might have several thinking processes about different matters. Thus, we assume that a person has at least two thinking processes about two different things within a certain period.

- A hypothetical single thinking process requires a goal point, one or many starting points (intentions to solve some specific problems), and one or many pieces of information (here written as "info point") connecting the starting points and the goal point. The info point represents the information used for solving particular problems.

- All required info points must be connected simultaneously to successfully reach the desired goal (producing the desired thought). In other words, a set only exists as it is upon having all of its elements. The mind does not know in advance which info points are required; thus, one needs to find them.

- There are shared info points among different thinking processes – think of one component being in different substances.

- The goals can be intended (as the desired result of active thinking) or unintended (not preset nor being aware by oneself).

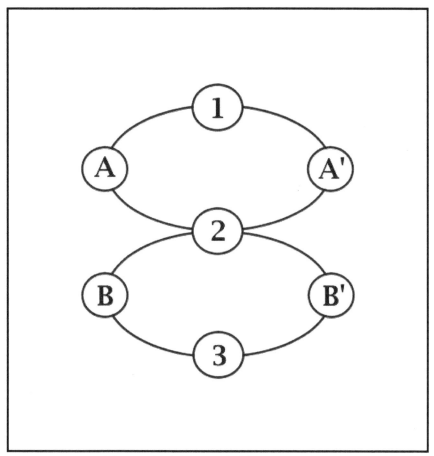

Figure 11.1: Two thinking processes

Based on these premises, a goal is deemed to be achieved (or a thought containing the values of the problem's solution is formed) when the information of the solution – treated as a set – contains all necessary values to solve the problem.

We consider two thinking processes in the following example (see Figure 10.1). Goal A′ requires info points (1) and (2); Goal B′ requires info points (2) and (3). Info point (2) is shared.

- Normal problem solving: Only process A-A′ with intended goal A′ happens. In this circumstance, one successfully finds info point (1) and (2) from the starting point A to achieve goal A′ (or solve problem A′).

- Serendipity type I (goal A′ being reached starting from B): One intends to solve two problems, A and B, in a similar period of time. In process A-A′ with the intended goal A′, they only find info point (1) when starting from A. In process B-B′ with unintended goal B′, they only find info point (2) when starting from B. Eventually, they acquire sufficient information to achieve goal A′ (or solve problem A′), while goal B′ has not been achieved.

- Serendipity type II (goal B′ being reached starting from A): In process A-A′ with the intended goal A′, only info point (2) was found starting from A. In process B-B′ with unintended goal B′, info point (3) has been found starting from B prior to process A-A′. Thus, when info point (2) is found in the process A-A′, it leads to the achievement of goal B′, while A′ has not been achieved.

- Serendipity type III (finding component values prior to setting goals): Process A-A′ has already been completed in advance. In other words, info points (1) and (2) have already been achieved. Goal B′ is initially unintended but later becomes intended because of the unexpected appearance of info point (3). Therefore, the combination of info points (2) and (3) helps achieve goal B′ (or solve problem B′).

Some further notes:

- The "unexpected" notion of the "missing piece" in the serendipity process is probably due to the different origin of that info point, which is found from a largely unrelated prior thought in relation to the starting point directly corresponding to the goal.

- In type III serendipity, goal A' is usually perceived by oneself as mundane or of low values compared to B', which creates the illusion of the info point (2) found starting from A "coming from nowhere".
- The perceived value of thoughts with unintended goals is unknown (default as neutral, or zero), and thus are more likely to be hastily discarded than thoughts with intended goals.
- When dealing with problems similar to the ones encountered before, we tend to try finding info points that were found to be useful (led to complete processes) in the past. Because we often employ ("old") thinking strategies based on known references, it may be difficult to find and integrate "novel" values – to be precise: trying new combinations of values.

It is important to note that at the moment, this non-linear thinking approach is still in early development, so it requires further theoretical expansion and empirical validation. Although some places are ambiguous, by presenting the preliminary explanation based on the non-linear information process here, we hope to share an interesting and potential research direction regarding serendipity.

11.3. Information exchange among social groups can help increase serendipity strike possibility

While coming up with new values and connecting information are skills, the factor of chance is conditional on the existence and accessibility to the information of interest (the "missing piece") within one's environment. However, as we have discussed throughout this book, a better understanding of serendipity's mechanism and properties can help carry out actions toward increasing the chance of its occurrence. The non-linear thinking approach shows that the serendipity strike for solving a particular problem usually comes from the information acquired from solving another problem (or access to a "novel" set of information). Thus, we argue that communication with other people in one's circle(s) can be helpful in this regard.

It is important to note that the "novelty" of a value or connection is subjective: a new approach or perspective in one person's eye can be something familiar in the eye of another. This means that information exchange between people (communication) is necessary. However, mindsets that are too different will make it more difficult to communicate effectively due to the low number of mutually shared perceived values. This means that we may want to focus on communicating with like-minded people, have similar levels of expertise, and have certain mutual purposes. These people are resource-rich in terms of valuable information concerning the topics of interest.

Additionally, due to the energy-saving mechanism of trust in subjective cost-benefit judgments (Le et al., 2021), information received from non-trusted sources, in general, has a lower rate of acceptance (Vuong et al., 2021b). Spending too much time and energy evaluating the trustworthiness of information sources can make the communication inefficient or even emotionally taxing. Thus, good scenarios for information exchange should be among those of close relationship (e.g., friends), having a relatively high level of shared knowledge and purposes on the topics of discussions (e.g., colleagues), but also approaching the topics by connecting different sets of values (e.g., from distinct personal experiences or perspectives).

This strategy for seeking breakthroughs has been employed quite naturally by humans since the earliest time of civilization and in various aspects of life. Each social circle often tends to share information and discuss its values among themselves: farmers on farming techniques, artists on the aesthetics, scientists on scientific investigations, philosophers on philosophical matters, etc. It is worth noting that information exchange in human society is not necessarily direct face-to-face conversations, but it can also happen through other forms of media such as written text or products of work (e.g., viewing art, examining machinery, or reading published papers).

The former chapter briefly mentioned Solvay Conferences' importance to modern physics and chemistry innovations. The activity of sharing ideas among top researchers in the fields can help facilitate the processes of novel value formulation and information connection. This kind of environment (e.g., at those conferences) has a high amount of useful information and new perspectives on the values of that information. If we think of serendipity as finding hidden treasure across the Seven Seas, this environment is an island filled with treasures. It is not surprising that innovations in every discipline often came from small groups of people with close connections.

From personal experiences, we have also come to realize that most of our serendipity moments leading to major works often resulted from some "sparks" during the informal meetings and chatting among ourselves. Several major studies of our team (the Centre for Interdisciplinary Social Research in Vietnam) are typical cases where serendipity holds a crucial role in creating the works (Nguyen et al., 2021, Nguyen, Le, & Khuc, 2021; Vuong, 2021; Vuong et al., 2018; Vuong et al., 2021a; Vuong et al., 2022). Furthermore, the main theories in this book also came from a serendipity strike that occurred to Dr. Vuong while he was reflecting on his childhood memories and the experiences of nature throughout his lifetime. Sometimes, we tell jokes that our best ideas may come from the weirdest topics in casual conversations. And thus, as a natural tendency, we often meet and talk among our small circle, not only because we are close friends and colleagues, but also because we know it can increase our chance of getting those valuable serendipity strikes.

Chapter references

Barber, B., & Fox, R. C. (1958). The case of the floppy-eared rabbits: an instance of serendipity gained and serendipity lost. *American Journal of Sociology, 64*(2), 128-136.

De Rond, M. (2014). The structure of serendipity. *Culture and Organization, 20*(5), 342-358.

Gothard, K. M. (2020). Multidimensional processing in the amygdala. *Nature Reviews Neuroscience, 21*(10), 565-575.

Le, T.-T., Nguyen, M.-H., & Vuong, Q.-H. (2021). Misinformation and the mindsponge mechanism of trust. *OSF Preprints.* https://osf.io/m9sj3

Napier, N., & Vuong, Q. H. (2013). Serendipity as a strategic advantage? In T. Wilkinson (Ed.), *Strategic management in the 21st century* (pp. 175-199). Praeger/ABC-Clio.

Nguyen, M.-H., & Vuong, Q.-H. (2021). Evaluation of the Aichi Biodiversity Targets: The international collaboration trilemma in interdisciplinary research. *Pacific Conservation Biology.* Online Early.

Nguyen, M.-H., Le, T.-T., & Khuc, Q. (2021). Bayesian Mindsponge Framework. *Scholarly Community Encyclopedia.* https://encyclopedia.pub/13852

Nguyen, M.-H., Le, T.-T., Nguyen, H.-K. T., Ho, M.-T., Nguyen, H. T. T., & Vuong, Q.-H. (2021). Alice in Suicideland: exploring the suicidal ideation mechanism through the sense of connectedness and help-seeking behaviors. *International Journal of Environmental Research and Public Health, 18*(7), 3681.

Stringer, C., Pachitariu, M., Steinmetz, N., Reddy, C. B., Carandini, M., & Harris, K. D. (2019). Spontaneous behaviors drive multidimensional, brainwide activity. *Science, 364*(6437), eaav7893.

Vuong, Q.-H. (2016). Global mindset as the integration of emerging socio-cultural values through mindsponge processes: A transition economy perspective. In J. Kuada (Ed.), *Global mindsets: exploration and perspectives* (pp. 109-126). Routledge.

Vuong, Q.-H. (2021). The semiconducting principle of monetary and environmental values exchange. *Economics and Business Letters, 10*(3), 284-290.

Vuong, Q.-H., & Napier, N. K. (2014). Making creativity: the value of multiple filters in the innovation process. *International Journal of Transitions and Innovation Systems, 3*(4), 294-327.

Vuong, Q.-H., & Napier, N. K. (2015). Acculturation and global mindsponge: an emerging market perspective. *International Journal of Intercultural Relations, 49*, 354-367.

Vuong, Q.-H., et al. (2018). Cultural additivity: behavioural insights from the interaction of Confucianism, Buddhism and Taoism in folktales. *Palgrave Communications, 4*, 143.

Vuong, Q.-H., Le, T.-T., La, V.-P., Nguyen, T. T. H., Ho, M.-T., Khuc, Q., & Nguyen, M.-H. (2022). Covid-19 vaccines production and societal immunization under the serendipity-mindsponge-3D knowledge management theory and conceptual framework. *Humanities and Social Sciences Communications, 9*, 22.

Vuong, Q.-H., Nguyen, M.-H., & Le, T.-T. (2021). *A mindsponge-based investigation into the psycho-religious mechanism behind suicide attacks*. Sciendo.

Vuong, Q.-H., Nguyen, M.-H., & Le, T.-T. (2021). Home scholarly culture, book selection reason, and academic performance: pathways to book reading interest among secondary school students. *European Journal of Investigation in Health, Psychology and Education, 11*(2), 468-495.

Hội An Ancient Town

©2021 Dam Thu Ha

Chapter 12:
Reflecting on the new theory of serendipity

Quan-Hoang Vuong

❧ • ❧

In this closing chapter, I summarize and reflect on all chapters' content from the beginning to the end. It has been a journey through personal insights, literature reviews, conceptualization, rationalization, and innovation. I revisit the main arguments about serendipity's conditionality and survival drivers and emphasize the importance of employing the mindsponge and 3D principles to maximize the chance of encountering serendipity and successfully capitalize on the phenomenon's outcomes. An integral serendipity-mindsponge-3D framework is demonstrated through my story about building the first national science databases. Additionally, some directions for future study on serendipity and its applications are suggested.

❧ • ❧

12.1. A journey through the book of a new serendipity theory

Many have regarded the phenomenon of serendipity almost as a mysterious "miracle". By treating serendipity as something coming from pure luck, one cannot be proactive in learning how to seek their "missing pieces". In other words, by giving the initiative to chance alone, one might lose more control over one's own intention. There are many things humans have not understood clearly, yet we still depend heavily on them in our everyday life (for example, think of our brain

https://doi.org/10.2478/9788366675865-018

functions and consciousness). While there will always be the unknown of the universe and the unexpectedness of life, understanding better influential phenomena will empower us by increasing our active role in problem-solving and decision-making. Considering the crucial role of serendipity in innovation throughout human history, it is clear that investigating the nature and mechanism of this particular phenomenon is very important; And that has been the aim and content of this book.

It began as a question lingering for ten years. I had been wondering about the causes and possible conditions of serendipity since I started working on the study of serendipity as a strategic advantage (Napier & Vuong, 2013). Time went by, but that question had always stayed in my mind. Until the day when I had a major moment of serendipity, and the core of this book was born.

Chapter 1 introduced how a book on serendipity is brought to life by serendipity. Here, serendipity is a concept seen not as luck but rather a product of a nurturing environment and the tireless work of a human mind. In Chapter 2, bibliometric analyses were conducted on 2982 serendipity-related documents retrieved from the Web of Science database. By examining the intellectual and conceptual structures in the field, we found three main research lines: 1) information-seeking behaviors, 2) serendipity in business and sciences, and 3) serendipity in recommender systems. We reviewed arguments about the definitions, types, influential factors, and processes of serendipity (André et al., 2009; Copeland, 2019; Cunha, 2005; Cunha et al., 2010; De Rond, 2014; Lawley & Tompkins, 2011; Makri & Blandford, 2012; McCay-Peet & Toms, 2010; McCay-Peet & Toms, 2015; Mendonça et al., 2008; Merton & Barber, 2004; Rubin et al., 2011).

In Chapter 3, I told stories about how the events of finding beautiful bird nests and observing strange bird behaviors had led to impactful scientific studies (Vuong, 2020, 2021a, 2021b). As demonstrated by the stories, serendipity is conditional, and it only comes if there exists the right question in one's mind, together with the suitable environment, expertise, and mindset. In Chapter 4, I talked about the survival aspects of serendipity through personal experiences with the medicinal plant mã đề, and the story of my daughter and the cicadas. Under numerous existential threats and constant environmental and social stress (Diamond, 2011), for humans, the skill to notice unexpected valuable information from their surroundings is crucial for survival. Serendipity can lead to innovations that give individuals or groups competitive advantages, helping them in the battle for "survival of the fittest" – a principle with its origin in Darwin's theory of evolution (Darwin, 2003). Innovations in, from, and for wars have pointed to this survival aspect of human society through the ages (Lee, 2016; Satia, 2019). Chapter 5 elaborated on serendipity's survival drivers divided into two categories of natural and social survival demands. We discussed some typical examples, from making fires and finding food in ancient eras to the rise of modern companies in competitive power. These survival demands underlying serendipity are closely related to Maslow's theory on humans' needs (Maslow, 1943).

Chapter 6 presented an in-depth theoretical analysis of our new theory of serendipity. According to this theory, serendipity is defined as an ability to notice, evaluate, and take advantage of unexpected information for survival purposes (both natural and social), of which the outcome and success rate are conditional on the individual (or organizational) mindset and environment. To increase our possibility of finding and making good use of serendipity, the mindsponge mechanism (Vuong & Napier, 2015; Vuong, 2016) and the 3D principles of creativity (Vuong & Napier, 2014). Creating a great innovation outcome requires employing all three factors of serendipity, mindsponge, and 3D in an integral system for optimal operation (Vuong et al., 2022). We went on to Chapter 7, discussing how to improve serendipity encounter and attainment probability. Here we introduced the concepts of the perceivable range, which determines the types of unexpectedness upon recognition by whether the key information is coming from within or outside one's range. Importantly, we presented six scenarios with serendipity encounter and attainment probability ranging from low to high. Briefly, the conditions differ by: 1) information available in the current environment, 2) whether the direction of seeking is right, 3) whether one follows a disciplined process or not, 4) the degree of open-mindedness, 5) whether one's knowledge and abilities for accurately evaluating the information is sufficient or not, and 6) whether the origin of the key information is from the external environment or the mind's buffer zone.

As the soul-touching element is a crucial factor throughout the serendipity process, Chapter 8 was dedicated to explaining the notion of the "soul factor" and how it contributes to the greatness of serendipity outcomes. The notion was clarified using some personal reflections on soul-touching research in humanities and social sciences. Chapter 9 revisited the case of floppy-eared rabbits with two researchers, where one successfully turned the unexpected information into an important scientific discovery while the other, given the same information, did not. These cases of serendipity gained and lost were analyzed through each step of the process using the new theory. In Chapter 10, we discussed building "pro-serendipity" environments and cultures. We briefly told the story of Ernest Solvay

– a scientist who greatly benefited from a serendipity moment, later contributed to building the environments for scientific information exchange, and institutes for nurturing future generations of scientists. The Solvay Conferences are associated with top scientists and their major innovations in physics and chemistry over the last century. Here, it is clear that the culture of science, which we all benefit from, deserves to be taken good care of (Vuong, 2018). Such "pro-serendipity" environments and organization cultures require a high density of both types of navigational and useful information – the former one for setting the right direction and the other for moving toward the goal.

Additionally, the act of navigating and moving should take turns smartly and regularly due to the chaotic and dynamic information flows of reality. It should also be noted that as a skill, serendipity might also be used for selfish purposes that may have unethical impacts, apart from innovations beneficial for humanities. Finally, Chapter 11 presented a preliminary theoretical development for exploring deeper into the information process of serendipity. We drew connections to possible non-linear thinking models. We again supported the notion that information exchange, in the right ways and the right environments, can help increase serendipity encounter and attainment possibility.

Through these chapters, the readers might get the answers for the nature, causes, and mechanism of serendipity, as well as the roles of the mindsponge mechanism and 3D process of creativity in the serendipity process. The serendipity-mindsponge-3D framework (SM3D) has supported me to accomplish various achievements throughout my career, including establishing the first national databases in Vietnam, so I hope it can also be helpful with others who read the book.

12.2. The SM3D framework in building the first Vietnamese national science databases

- **From a personal background**

Those were the mid-summer nights from my childhood, in the late 1970s, when the buzzing sound of cicadas overpowered the sweaty air, and we children, mosquito nets in hands, set out for our scientific inquiry. We would roam around late evening in search of juvenile cicadas and, in utter silence, holding our breath, watch how the insect wiggles and sheds its outer shell before spreading its transparent wings and taking flights. The enchanting moment was filled with our noisy debate about what happened and why. Every time, the curiosity in me would soon be overtaken by an inexplicable sentiment — these cicadas are, in fact, so fragile and short-lived that they would all be gone after a few weeks of singing.

From a young age, I have long been interested in observing natural phenomena and recording bits and bits of data, whether it be the number of metamorphoses we saw a night or the time it took for one to completely transform and fly away. The memories have stayed with me as I took on different career paths, all of which are rooted in curiosity to explain today's data-centric world. Since I published my first academic paper in 1997, I have done work for universities, governments, and industries and started my own businesses. My main work has involved data preparation, database design and construction, data-processing applications, and data analysis. These experiences have allowed me to observe the remarkable parallels in the seemingly "impossible triangle" of nature, academia, and entrepreneurship (see Figure 12.1).

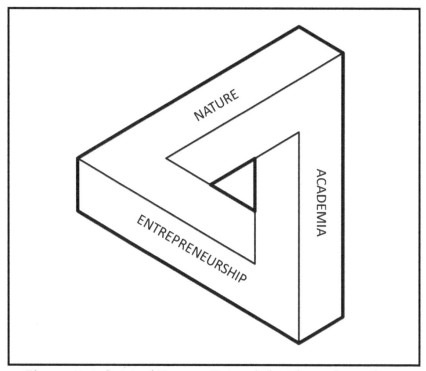

Figure 12.1: Original Penrose Triangle by Lluisa Iborra from the Noun Project (Iborra, n.d.); Reformulated triangle with texts under Creative Commons CC BY license by Quan-Hoang Vuong.

In the middle of this impossible triangle, data coherently rationalizes and weaves nature, academia, and entrepreneurship. Even though I did not have any idea during those mid-summer nights, the patient observation of cicadas is a form of data collection. While the data that I collected back then was used for noisy debates with friends, in a way, they prepared me for my long career in business and academia. In 2017, I founded a database named SSHPA to systematically analyze Vietnamese social scientists' research capacity since 2008 to aid science policymaking (Vuong et al., 2018). Later, the project was funded by

Vietnam's National Foundation for Science and Technology Development (NAFOSTED). Later, I co-founded another database that covers 80 years of mathematic development in Vietnam, with its code name being "SciMath DB," with Prof. Ngô Bảo Châu (a 2010 Fields Medalist), the Vietnamese mathematician of the University of Chicago—awarded the top mathematics honor together with the French mathematician Cédric Villani. Prof. Ngô Bảo Châu initiated the SciMath DB Project as Scientific Director of the Vietnam Institute for Advanced Study in Mathematics (VIASM).

Here, it can be said that the conditions for future possible serendipity moments are built upon personal experiences even since one's childhood. The living environments and the culture one lives in all matter in establishing the mindset. All these experiences later helped me notice the opportunities for establishing the national science databases.

- **Scavenging resources, with the right timing and serendipity**

Both academics and entrepreneurs will find that timing and serendipity often define successes and failures (Vuong, 2016, 2019). The key is to have the right mindset to catch and nurture those serendipity moments and their values. For example, in late 2016, seeing that science policymakers were at a crossroads of revamping domestic research capacity in line with international standards, I realized that, with my limited resources, this was the only window of possibility to build the SSHPA database (Vuong et al., 2018). The primary reasons were the small number of Vietnamese authors with international publications at the time, which made it feasible to track and verify each record, and the potential for commercialization. Having confidence in one's ideas and seizing the opportunity enables us to maximize our chance for career advancement and social impacts.

Eventually, the SSHPA database also impacted the Vietnam Ministry of Education and Training's Circular 08, which requires Ph.D. candidates, and their supervisors to publish their works internationally in 2017 (Nguyen et al., 2019). Such a meaningful data-policy interaction has encouraged me to continue the journey.

Both academics and entrepreneurs often start with very little resources; thus, managing and growing limited resources is a key question of survival (Vuong, 2018; Vuong, 2020). Such survival demands are the drivers for asking the questions that may lead to innovations. The most important resource, for me, are ideas and mindsets. Finding the right ideas and having the right mindsets allow you to organically attract the right people and grow your organization. Thus, in 2017, I assembled a team of four young graduates for the SSHPA database (Vuong et al., 2018). I trained the team members from the baby steps of data identification, collection, storage, organization, categorization to the more complicated tasks of software engineering support and database system management. With our core values defined, early investment in human capital proves to be vital for the long-term sustainability of the academic enterprise.

Letting the young graduates face the endlessness of data in databases such as SSHPA or SciMath is mental preparation for scientific research's hardship. They offer a unique insight into the nature of science, especially social sciences. Some problems need to be addressed. Some thoughts need to be jotted down. Some reviews need to be rebutted. It resonates deeply with the image of Sisyphus that Albert Camus used to conceptualize the absurdity (Camus, 2013). As his eternal punishment, Sisyphus had to push a rock up a mountain so it could roll back down again. For eternity, he does it over and over again. Through interaction with data, the young graduates can confront the endlessness, embrace it, continuously learn and unlearn, and find happiness from such an absurd condition (Vuong, 2016). This courage of conviction is very important to find like-minded colleagues and build a culture for a research team.

Here, we can see the role of creating an environment rich in both navigational information (instructions and experiences from seniors) and useful information (available sources of knowledge and protocols). The social survival drive is fueled by encountering challenges. The culture of science being built also aims at nurturing curiosity and experiments, which are crucial for innovation. Information exchange is facilitated within the group, increasing the chance to connect new values and perspectives. The young team members and I must process a considerable amount of new information through each project and update our mindsets accordingly, following the mindsponge mechanism (Vuong & Napier, 2015; Vuong et al., 2021).

- **Courage and perseverance to walk the dark road**

It might be a cliché, but both academics and entrepreneurs find the most success when they have the courage to walk the untrodden path, climb the mountains, and go the extra mile. Again, it is the survival desire that drives humans' creativity. When Ngô Bảo Châu and I decided in 2017 to build the SciMath database, we did not have any funding. All we had was the glorious tradition and history of Vietnam mathematics with keen interest and engagement from well-known figures such as Laurent Schwartz (1915-2002; 1950 Fields Medalist) and Alexander Grothendieck (1928-2014; 1966 Fields Medalist), or Hoàng Tụy's (1927-2019; 2011 Constantin Carathéodory Prize) internationally recognized pioneering work on global optimization, which brought him the honor of the "Tuy cuts" (Tuy, 1968) and the "DC

Programming" (Tuy, 1986). We decided to follow our entrepreneurial instinct and self-funded the project while waiting for the right investor or business partner to come.

Figure 12.2: A graphical presentation of Vietnamese mathematicians' network from 2010-2021, extracted from the SciMath Database as of March 10, 2021 (Chau et al., 2020).

Three years in, not only have we secured sufficient funding from the private sector, but we have also completed collecting electronic records of more than 10,000 indexed mathematic papers (co-)written by Vietnamese authors (Chau et al., 2020). To be exact, as of March 10,

2021, the SciMath database has recorded 10,475 papers, 74 years, and 1,995 mathematicians.

The data count can feel lifeless, but they were contributed by papers written in bloody wars from the 1940s to the 1970s, political conflicts, economic and communication barriers (Thiem, 1949, 1950; Tuy, 1968). Figure 12.2 demonstrates the network of Vietnamese mathematicians from 2010 until 2021.

In this sense, I see the project very much like a banyan tree, which takes years to set its deep roots and grow out its massive trunk and branches. The data walks us through the works of many intellectual architects and how they set Vietnamese mathematics's roots. Hoàng Tụy and Lê Văn Thiêm, for instance, initiated the Institute of Mathematics, the cradle for the career of many influential Vietnamese mathematicians. We learned how Ngô Bảo Châu's recipient of the Fields medals set a new milestone in mathematical research, how the event gave people the courage to climb the academic ladder. Figure 12.3 presents the number of mathematic articles ten years before Ngô Bảo Châu's achievement (2000-2010) and ten years after (2011-2020). From 2000 until 2010, only 2531 articles were recorded. The number of mathematics articles doubled in the next 10-year period with 4474 articles. The achievement of Ngô Bảo Châu also allowed enormous resources to be invested in mathematics. The most notable being the National Key Program on Mathematics Development in the 2011-2020 period (Vietnam Government, 2010). The Prime Minister approved the program under Decision No. 1483/QD-TTg, with the funding of VND 651 billion (approximately USD 28.5 million).

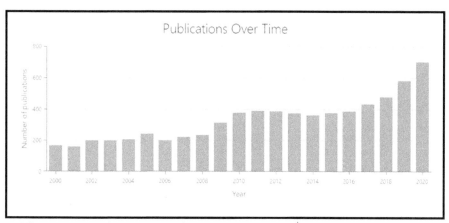

Figure 12.3: The output of Vietnam mathematics before and after Ngô Bảo Châu's Fields medal in 2010.

Besides providing an overview of the mathematical research in Vietnam, the SciMath database can also help policymakers identify research gaps, rising mathematicians, or strong research centers. For instance, the SciMath database has identified 23 out of 1995 Vietnamese authors with publications in top mathematics journals (see Table 12.1). The information will be crucial for policymakers in the future, just as in the case of the SSHPA database and Circular 08.

Table 12.1: Mathematics authors with articles in top mathematics journals

Author	Number of articles	Number of top journals
Pham Huu Tiep	21	6
Vu Ha Van	17	5
Duong Hong Phong	13	6
Dinh Tien Cuong	6	5
Ngo Bao Chau	6	4
Ngo Viet Trung	6	3
Lu Hoang Chinh	5	4

Nguyen Hoai Minh	4	4
Nguyen Trong Toan	3	2
Nguyen Huu Hoi	2	2
Nguyen Sum	2	1
Nguyen Duy Tan	2	1
Pham Hoang Hiep	2	2
Pham Hung Quy	2	1
Pham Ngoc Anh	1	1
Phung Ho Hai	1	1
Nguyen Huu Anh	1	1
Nguyen Tien Dung	1	1
Nguyen Van Hoang	1	1
Nguyen Cong Minh	1	1
Nguyen Dang Hop	1	1
Dao Hai Long	1	1
Ha Huy Khoai	1	1
Le Van Thiem	1	1

The dataset, insights, and remaining unanswered questions have contributed to the national policymakers' decisions to continue government funding to the project and reaffirm support to VIASM in the next ten years. In order to reach this success, besides expertise, experience, flexibility, and innovation, we also followed a disciplined process in our work, as presented in the 3D principles of creativity (Vuong & Napier, 2014).

- **Risk management, goal setting, and the big picture**

To survive and thrive, both an academic and an entrepreneur must learn to manage risks, set goals, deal with inevitable setbacks in their journeys. In my experience of building two large databases understanding the different levels of risk involved in each project, I learned the importance of choosing a challenge that matches our potential with 80 years of data for the SciMath project posing a more daunting prospect the time. For this reason, we kicked off the SSHPA project first in 2017, ensuring that our system could handle ten years' worth of data before embarking on the more ambitious project of SciMath in early 2020. Continually testing one's growing capacity contributes to cultivating a sustainable research culture.

Moreover, as the young graduates grow with the process of data collection, it is important for them to reflect on their own journeys. Certainly, while big projects like SSHPA or SciMath can be a project for veteran researchers, they can mean a lot for young researchers. Working on the projects amid the reproducibility crisis (Munafò et al., 2017), the young graduates can deeply understand the importance of data. The trickiness of a situation when the findings will never be corrected unless the authors or someone else realize that something is off cannot be taught easily without working with data firsthand (Haas, 2021).

In a world where even basic facts get repeatedly questioned (Kata, 2010; Vuong, 2021), I often think back on how I have arrived at countless moments of truth by observing nature and curiosity in science. The transient nature of life is perhaps something we all think about from time to time. As I relive the summer nights and the cicada metamorphosis at fifty years old, I also reflect on my journey as an academic entrepreneur. Like a pendulum, the journey finds equilibrium in asking questions and finding answers by collecting data and using an appropriate scientific method.

As I have learned, building an academic enterprise means finding the elusive answers in the deluge of data and social problems today. This is all the more relevant as uncertainty from the COVID-19 pandemic continues to envelop our world (Huynh, 2020; Pham & Ho, 2020). Vaccine development, production, and distribution are typical innovative information processes on a global scale that integrate all aspects of the serendipity-mindsponge-3D framework (Vuong et al., 2022). Additionally, social scientists can create various products and services from the raw social data streams. In doing so, we bring our expertise to bear on the great task of finding much-needed social innovations for our social structures, which have been subjected to the break-neck speed of computational development.

Last but not least, as a senior researcher, I also think about paying it forward. Hopefully, the kind of academic enterprise that we build can ease some of the struggles early-career researchers face, sowing the seeds for a healthy academic ecosystem for the next generations and their future innovations.

12.3. The way onward

Throughout this book, we have looked at various angles on the new serendipity concept with complex conditionality and underlying multi-level survival motives. Based on these insights, we can expand their applications in various directions and disciplines. Again, it is important to note that serendipity on its own likely will not lead to considerable impacts; rather, employing the frameworks of mindsponge information processing and the 3D principles of creativity is necessary for practicality (on both individual and organizational levels). Our presented concepts and models of serendipity-mindsponge-3D are quite flexible and potentially applicable in many different situations. Scientists from all disciplines and interested experts from other fields are more than welcome to discuss and provide constructive criticism on the theory of serendipity presented in this book and validate or expand its practical applications. For example, further studies on serendipity's conditionality and survival aspect can benefit from collaborations among neuroscience, psychology, sociology, and anthropology. Information processing research can further explore the information mechanism of serendipity, creative thinking, or general problem-solving. Practical applications can be expanded on various issues, such as building an organizational culture to promote innovation, supporting creativity in education, or even self-help strategies to improve one's innovativeness and productivity.

Compared to our ancestors, humans in modern society better understand the nature of objects and phenomena found in our surrounding environments. That understanding did not make the natural world any less beautiful and awe-inspiring; rather, it helps us appreciate Mother Earth, the vast universe, as well as the complex human mind even more. We have come to know more about how much we are yet to know, and richer knowledge makes us more curious. Similarly, a clearer insight into the nature, emergence, and mechanism of serendipity will not make its moment any less miraculous; rather, we will appreciate even more the efforts of everyone put into building every necessary condition that has led to that very moment of "unexpectedness", because we know it cannot just be mere happenstance. Serendipity has now been another step closer to our understanding, and with it, creativity may lead the way to a better future for humanity.

Chapter references

André, P., Schraefel, M., Teevan, J., & Dumais, S. T. (2009). Discovery is never by chance: designing for (un)serendipity. *Proceedings of the Seventh ACM Conference on Creativity and Cognition*, 305-314.

Camus, A. (2013). *The myth of Sisyphus*. Penguin UK (Originally published in 1942).

Chau, N. B., Hoang, V. Q., Phuong, L. V., Hoa, L. T., Ha, L. M., Giang, T. T. T., ... Toan, H. M. (2020). *The 80-year development of Vietnam mathematical research: Preliminary insights from the SciMath database on mathematicians, their works and their networks*. Technical Report No. VIASM-AISDL-20.02, presented at VIASM Scientific Council Meeting on November 13, 2020. Retrieved from (January 10, 2022) https://arxiv.org/abs/2011.09328

Copeland, S. (2019). On serendipity in science: discovery at the intersection of chance and wisdom. *Synthese, 196*(6), 2385-2406.

Cunha, M. P. (2005). Serendipity: why some organizations are luckier than others. *FEUNL Working Paper Series*, 472.

Cunha, M. P. E., Clegg, S. R., & Mendonça, S. (2010). On serendipity and organizing. *European Management Journal, 28*(5), 319-330.

Darwin, C. (2003). *On the origin of species* (D. Knight, Ed. Reprint ed.). Routledge.

De Rond, M. (2014). The structure of serendipity. *Culture and Organization, 20*(5), 342-358.

Diamond, J. M. (2011). *Collapse: how societies choose to fail or survive*. Penguin Books.

Haas, B. D. (2021). What my retraction taught me. *Nature, 589*, 331.

Huynh, T. L. D. (2020). Does culture matter social distancing under the COVID-19 pandemic? *Safety Science, 130,* 104872.

Iborra, L. (n.d.). *Penrose Triangle.* The Noun Project. Retrieved from (March 10, 2021) https://thenounproject.com/search/?creator=2129742&q=Penrose&i=881121

Kata, A. (2010). A postmodern Pandora's box: Anti-vaccination misinformation on the Internet. *Vaccine, 28*(7), 1709-1716.

Lawley, J., & Tompkins, P. (2011). *Maximising serendipity: the art of recognising and fostering unexpected potential - A systemic approach to change.* The Clean Collection. Retrieved from https://cleanlanguage.co.uk/articles/articles/224/1/Maximising-Serendipity/Page1.html (accessed on: December 31, 2021)

Lee, W. E. (2016). *Waging war: conflict, culture, and innovation in world history.* Oxford University Press.

Makri, S., & Blandford, A. (2012). Coming across information serendipitously–Part 1: A process model. *Journal of Documentation, 68*(5), 684-705.

Maslow, A. H. (1943). A theory of human motivation. *Psychological Review, 50*(4), 370-396.

McCay-Peet, L., & Toms, E. G. (2010). The process of serendipity in knowledge work. *Proceedings of the Third Symposium on Information Interaction in Context,* 377-382.

McCay-Peet, L., & Toms, E. G. (2015). Investigating serendipity: How it unfolds and what may influence it. *Journal of the Association for Information Science and Technology, 66*(7), 1463-1476.

Mendonça, S., Cunha, M., & Clegg, S. R. (2008). Unsought innovation: serendipity in organizations. Entrepreneurship and Innovation—Organizations, Institutions, Systems and Regions Conference, Copenhagen.

Merton, R. K., & Barber, E. (2004). *The travels and adventures of serendipity: a study in sociological semantics and the sociology of science*. Princeton University Press.

Munafò, M. R., Nosek, B. A., Bishop, D. V. M., Button, K. S., Chambers, C. D., Percie du Sert, N., ... Ioannidis, J. P. A. (2017). A manifesto for reproducible science. *Nature Human Behaviour, 1*, 0021.

Napier, N., & Vuong, Q. H. (2013). Serendipity as a strategic advantage? In T. Wilkinson (Ed.), *Strategic management in the 21st century* (pp. 175-199). Praeger/ABC-Clio.

Nguyen, H.-K. T., Nguyen, T.-H. T., Ho, M.-T., Ho, M.-T., & Vuong, Q.-H. (2019). Scientific publishing: the point of no return. In Q. H. Vuong & T. Trung (Eds.), *The Vietnamese Social Sciences at a Fork in the Road* (pp. 143-162). De Gruyter.

Pham, H.-H., & Ho, T.-T.-H. (2020). Toward a 'new normal' with e-learning in Vietnamese higher education during the post COVID-19 pandemic. *Higher Education Research & Development, 39*(7), 1327–1331.

Rubin, V. L., Burkell, J., & Quan-Haase, A. (2011). Facets of serendipity in everyday chance encounters: a grounded theory approach to blog analysis. *Information Research, 16*(3), 488.

Satia, P. (2019). *Empire of guns: the violent making of the Industrial Revolution*. Stanford University Press.

Thiem, L.-V. (1949). Über das Umkehrproblem der Wertverteilungslehre. *Commentarii Mathematici Helvetici, 23*(1), 26-49.

Thiem, L.-V. (1950). Sur un problème d'inversion dans la théorie des fonctions méromorphes. *Annales scientifiques de l'É.NS, 3e*(67), 51-98.

Tuy, H. (1968). On linear inequalities. (English. Russian original). *Soviet Mathematics. Doklady, 9*, 366-369.

Tuy, H. (1986). A general deterministic approach to global optimization VIA D.C. Programming. In J. B. Hiriart-Urruty (Ed.), *North-Holland Mathematics Studies* (Vol. 129, pp. 273-303). North-Holland.

Vietnam Government. (2010). *Decision No. 1483/QD-TTg dated August 17, 2010, of the Prime Minister approving the national key program on mathematics development in the 2010-2020 period*. Viet Nam Government Portal. Retrieved from (March 11, 2021).

Vuong, Q. H. (2016). Global mindset as the integration of emerging socio-cultural values through mindsponge processes: A transition economy perspective. In: J. Kuada (Ed.), *Global mindsets: exploration and perspectives* (pp. 109-126). Routledge.

Vuong, Q. H., & Napier, N. K. (2014). Making creativity: the value of multiple filters in the innovation process. *International Journal of Transitions and Innovation Systems, 3*(4), 294-327.

Vuong, Q.-H. (2018). The (ir)rational consideration of the cost of science in transition economies. *Nature Human Behaviour, 2*, 5.

Vuong, Q.-H. (2019). Breaking barriers in publishing demands a proactive attitude. *Nature Human Behaviour, 3*, 1034.

Vuong, Q.-H. (2020). From children's literature to sustainability science, and young scientists for a more sustainable Earth. *Journal of Sustainability Education, 24*(3), 1-12. http://www.susted.com/wordpress/content/from-childrens-literature-to-sustainability-science-and-young-scientists-for-a-more-sustainable-earth_2020_12/

Vuong, Q.-H. (2021a). The semiconducting principle of monetary and environmental values exchange. *Economics and Business Letters, 10*(3), 284-290.

Vuong, Q.-H. (2021b). Western monopoly of climate science is creating an eco-deficit culture. *Economy, Land & Climate Insight*. https://elc-insight.org/western-monopoly-of-climate-science-is-creating-an-eco-deficit-culture/

Vuong, Q.-H., & Napier, N. K. (2015). Acculturation and global mindsponge: an emerging market perspective. *International Journal of Intercultural Relations, 49*, 354-367.

Vuong, Q.-H., La, V.-P., Vuong, T.-T., Ho, M.-T., Nguyen, H.-K. T., Nguyen, V.-H., ... Ho, M.-T. (2018). An open database of productivity in Vietnam's social sciences and humanities for public use. *Scientific Data, 5*, 180188.

Vuong, Q.-H., Le, T.-T., La, V.-P., Nguyen, T. T. H., Ho, M.-T., Khuc, Q., & Nguyen, M.-H. (2022). Covid-19 vaccines production and societal immunization under the serendipity-mindsponge-3D knowledge management theory and conceptual framework. *Humanities and Social Sciences Communications, 9*, 22.

Kingfisher

©2020 Dam Thu Ha

Book references

Adam, D. (2021). How far will global population rise? Researchers can't agree. *Nature, 597*, 462-465.

Alleva, L. (2006). Taking time to savour the rewards of slow science. *Nature, 443*(7109), 271.

Andel, P. v. (1994). Anatomy of the unsought finding. Serendipity: Origin, history, domains, traditions, appearances, patterns and programmability. *The British Journal for the Philosophy of Science, 45*(2), 631-648.

Anderson, W. A., Banerjee, U., Drennan, C. L., Elgin, S. C. R., Epstein, I. R., Handelsman, J., ... Warner, I. M. (2011). Changing the culture of science education at research universities. *Science, 331*(6014), 152-153.

Andrade, T. (2017). *The gunpowder age: China, military innovation, and the rise of the West in world history*. Princeton University Press.

André, P., Schraefel, M., Teevan, J., & Dumais, S. T. (2009). Discovery is never by chance: designing for (un) serendipity. *Proceedings of the Seventh ACM Conference on Creativity and Cognition*, 305-314.

Barber, B., & Fox, R. C. (1958). The case of the floppy-eared rabbits: An instance of serendipity gained and serendipity lost. *American Journal of Sociology, 64*(2), 128-136.

Bates, S. (2017). Literature Listing. *World Patent Information, 48*, 29-41.

Bates, S. (2019). Literature Listing. *World Patent Information, 57*, 41-54.

Bates, S. (2020). Literature Listing. *World Patent Information, 61*, 101963.

Belfort, J. (2007). *The Wolf of Wall Street*. Bantam Books.

https://doi.org/10.2478/9788366675865-019

Bergström, A., Stringer, C., Hajdinjak, M., Scerri, E. M. L., & Skoglund, P. (2021). Origins of modern human ancestry. *Nature, 590,* 229-237.

Berkun, S. (2010). *The Myths of Innovation.* O'Reilly.

Birnbaum, J. (2022). *Why video game makers see huge potential in Blockchain—and why problems loom for their new NFTs.* Forbes. Retrieved from (January 11, 2022) https://www.forbes.com/sites/justinbirnbaum/2022/01/06/why -video-game-makers-see-huge-potential-in-blockchain-and- why-problems-loom-for-their-new-nfts/?sh=6abd10f043d7

Björneborn, L. (2008). Serendipity dimensions and users' information behaviour in the physical library interface. *Information Research, 13*(4), 370.

Braun, D. R., Aldeias, V., Archer, W., Arrowsmith, J. R., Baraki, N., Campisano, C. J., ... Reed, K. E. (2019). Earliest known Oldowan artifacts at >2.58 Ma from Ledi-Geraru, Ethiopia, highlight early technological diversity. *Proceedings of the National Academy of Sciences, 116*(24), 11712-11717.

Brown, S. (2005). Science, serendipity and the contemporary marketing condition. *European Journal of Marketing, 39*(11/12), 1229-1234.

Camus, A. (2013). *The myth of Sisyphus.* Penguin UK (Originally published in 1942).

Charlton, B. G., & Walston, F. (2002). Individual case studies in clinical research. *Journal of Evaluation in Clinical Practice, 4*(2), 147-155.

Chase, K. (2003). *Firearms: A global history to 1700.* Cambridge University Press.

Chau, N. B., Hoang, V. Q., Phuong, L. V., Hoa, L. T., Ha, L. M., Giang, T. T. T., ... Toan, H. M. (2020). *The 80-year development of*

Vietnam mathematical research: Preliminary insights from the SciMath database on mathematicians, their works and their networks. Technical Report No. VIASM-AISDL-20.02, presented at VIASM Scientific Council Meeting on November 13, 2020. Retrieved from (January 10, 2022) https://arxiv.org/abs/2011.09328

Chiến, B. N., & Hoàng, V. Q. (2015). *Bằng chứng cuộc sống: Suy ngẫm về phát triển bền vững Việt Nam.* NXB Chính trị Quốc gia Sự Thật.

Choi, C. (2016). Ancient Chinese may have cultivated grass seeds 30,000 years ago. *PNAS Journal Club.* https://blog.pnas.org/2016/03/journal-club-ancient-chinese-may-have-cultivated-grass-seeds-30000-years-ago/

Clark, T. J. (2013). *Picasso and truth: from Cubism to Guernica* (Vol. 56). Princeton University Press.

Copeland, S. (2019). On serendipity in science: discovery at the intersection of chance and wisdom. *Synthese, 196*(6), 2385-2406.

Cunha, M. P. (2005). Serendipity: why some organizations are luckier than others. *FEUNL Working Paper Series,* 472.

Cunha, M. P. e., Clegg, S. R., & Mendonça, S. (2010). On serendipity and organizing. *European Management Journal, 28*(5), 319-330.

Curtin, N. J. (2020). The development of Rucaparib/Rubraca®: A story of the synergy between science and serendipity. *Cancers, 12*(3), 564.

Darwin, C. (2003). *On the origin of species* (D. Knight, Ed. Reprint ed.). Routledge.

Dasgupta, S. (2019). The complexity of creativity: Les Demoiselles D'Avignon as a cognitive-historical laboratory. *Creativity Research Journal, 31*(4), 377-394.

De Rond, M. (2014). The structure of serendipity. *Culture and Organization, 20*(5), 342-358.

Delcourt, M. A. (2003). Five ingredients for success: two case studies of advocacy at the state level. *Gifted Child Quarterly, 47*(1), 26-37.

Denrell, J., Fang, C., & Winter, S. G. (2003). The economics of strategic opportunity. *Strategic Management Journal, 24*(10), 977-990.

Dew, N. (2009). Serendipity in entrepreneurship. *Organization Studies, 30*(7), 735-753.

Diamond, J. M. (2011). *Collapse: how societies choose to fail or survive.* Penguin Books.

Diaz de Chumaceiro, C. L. (2004). Serendipity and pseudoserendipity in career paths of successful women: Orchestra conductors. *Creativity Research Journal, 16*(2-3), 345-356.

Đỗ, T. L. (2015). *Những cây thuốc và vị thuốc Việt Nam* (19 ed.). NXB Hồng Đức.

Eisenhardt, K. M. (1989). Building theories from case study research. *Academy of Management Review, 14*(4), 532-550.

Ekins, S., Diaz, N., Chung, J., Mathews, P., & McMurtray, A. (2017). Enabling anyone to translate clinically relevant ideas to therapies. *Pharmaceutical Research, 34*(1), 1-6.

Fine, G. A., & Deegan, J. G. (1996). Three principles of Serendip: insight, chance, and discovery in qualitative research. *International Journal of Qualitative Studies in Education, 9*(4), 434-447.

Fink, T. M. A., Reeves, M., Palma, R., & Farr, R. S. (2017). Serendipity and strategy in rapid innovation. *Nature Communications, 8,* 2002.

Fisberg, M., & Machado, R. (2015). History of yogurt and current patterns of consumption. *Nutrition Reviews, 73*(suppl_1), 4-7.

Forbes. (2021). *Howard Schultz*. Forbes. Retrieved from (January 11, 2022) https://www.forbes.com/profile/howard-schultz/

Foster, A., & Ford, N. (2003). Serendipity and information seeking: an empirical study. *Journal of Documentation, 59*(3), 321-340.

Gaglio, C. M., & Katz, J. A. (2001). The psychological basis of opportunity identification: Entrepreneurial alertness. *Small Business Economics, 16*(2), 95-111.

Ge, M., Delgado-Battenfeld, C., & Jannach, D. (2010). Beyond accuracy: evaluating recommender systems by coverage and serendipity. *Proceedings of the Fourth ACM Conference on Recommender Systems*, 257-260.

Gilbert, E. (2016). *Big magic: creative living beyond fear*. Riverhead Books.

Ginsburg, A. S., & Klugman, K. P. (2020). COVID-19 pneumonia and the appropriate use of antibiotics. *The Lancet Global Health, 8*(12), e1453-e1454.

Gothard, K. M. (2020). Multidimensional processing in the amygdala. *Nature Reviews Neuroscience, 21*(10), 565-575.

Gowlett, J. A. J. (2016). The discovery of fire by humans: a long and convoluted process. *Philosophical Transactions of the Royal Society B: Biological Sciences, 371*(1696).

Grivtsova, L. Y., Falaleeva, N. A., & Tupitsyn, N. N. (2021). Azoximer Bromide: mystery, serendipity, and promise. *Frontiers in Oncology, 11*, 699546.

Haas, B. D. (2021). What my retraction taught me. *Nature, 589*, 331.

Hart, R. A. (2013). *Children's participation: the theory and practice of involving young citizens in community development and environmental care*. Routledge.

Harvey, F. (2021). Climate experts warn world leaders 1.5C is 'real science', not just talking point. *The Guardian*. Retrieved from

(January 11, 2022)

https://www.theguardian.com/environment/2021/oct/30/clima
te-experts-warn-world-leaders-15c-is-real-science-not-just-
talking-point

Herlocker, J. L., Konstan, J. A., Terveen, L. G., & Riedl, J. T. (2004).
Evaluating collaborative filtering recommender systems.
ACM Transactions on Information Systems, 22(1), 5-53.

Holman, L., Head, M. L., Lanfear, R., & Jennions, M. D. (2015).
Evidence of experimental bias in the life sciences: why we
need blind data recording. *PLoS Biology, 13*(7), e1002190.

Huynh, T. L. D. (2020). Does culture matter social distancing under
the COVID-19 pandemic? *Safety Science, 130*, 104872.

Iborra, L. (n.d.). *Penrose Triangle*. The Noun Project. Retrieved from
(March 10, 2021)
https://thenounproject.com/search/?creator=2129742&q=Penro
se&i=881121

International Dairy Foods Association. (2021). *History of cheese*.
International Dairy Foods Association. Retrieved from
https://www.idfa.org/news-views/media-kits/cheese/history-
of-cheese (accessed on: January 11, 2022)

Jiang, S., Li, Y., Lu, Q., Hong, Y., Guan, D., Xiong, Y., & Wang, S.
(2021). Policy assessments for the carbon emission flows and
sustainability of Bitcoin blockchain operation in China. *Nature
Communications, 12*, 1938.

Kata, A. (2010). A postmodern Pandora's box: Anti-vaccination
misinformation on the Internet. *Vaccine, 28*(7), 1709-1716.

Kames, J., Holcomb, D. D., Kimchi, O., DiCuccio, M., Hamasaki-
Katagiri, N., Wang, T., ... Kimchi-Sarfaty, C. (2020). Sequence
analysis of SARS-CoV-2 genome reveals features important
for vaccine design. *Scientific Reports, 10*(1), 15643.

Kellner, A., & Robertson, T. (1954). Selective necrosis of cardiac and skeletal muscle induced experimentally by means of proteolytic enzyme solutions given intravenously. *The Journal of Experimental Medicine, 99*(4), 387-404.

Kellner, A., Robertson, T., & Mott, H. (1951). Blood coagulation defect induced in rabbits by papain solutions injected intravenously. *Federation Proceedings, 10*(1).

Kolbert, E. (2014). *The sixth extinction: an unnatural history* (First edition ed.). Henry Holt and Company.

Kotkov, D., Wang, S., & Veijalainen, J. (2016). A survey of serendipity in recommender systems. *Knowledge-based systems, 111*, 180-192.

Krause, M. J., & Tolaymat, T. (2018). Quantification of energy and carbon costs for mining cryptocurrencies. *Nature Sustainability, 1*(11), 711-718.

La, V.-P., & Vuong, Q.-H. (2019). bayesvl: Visually learning the graphical structure of Bayesian networks and performing MCMC with 'Stan'. *The Comprehensive R Archive Network (CRAN)*.

Lawley, J., & Tompkins, P. (2011). *Maximising serendipity: The art of recognising and fostering unexpected potential - A systemic approach to change*. The Clean Collection. Retrieved from https://cleanlanguage.co.uk/articles/articles/224/1/Maximising -Serendipity/Page1.html (accessed on: December 31, 2021)

Le, T.-T., Nguyen, M.-H., & Vuong, Q.-H. (2021). Misinformation and the mindsponge mechanism of trust. *OSF Preprints*. https://osf.io/m9sj3

Lee, W. E. (2016). *Waging war: conflict, culture, and innovation in world history*. Oxford University Press.

Levy, O., Beechler, S., Taylor, S., & Boyacigiller, N. A. (2007). What we talk about when we talk about 'global mindset': managerial cognition in multinational corporations. *Journal of International Business Studies, 38*(2), 231-258.

Makri, S., & Blandford, A. (2012). Coming across information serendipitously–Part 1: A process model. *Journal of Documentation, 68*(5), 684-705.

Makri, S., Blandford, A., Woods, M., Sharples, S., & Maxwell, D. (2014). "Making my own luck": serendipity strategies and how to support them in digital information environments. *Journal of the Association for Information Science and Technology, 65*(11), 2179-2194.

Maslow, A. H. (1943). A theory of human motivation. *Psychological Review, 50*(4), 370-396.

Maslow, A. H. (1981). *Motivation and personality.* Prabhat Prakashan.

McBirnie, A. (2008). Seeking serendipity: the paradox of control. *Aslib Proceedings, 60*(6), 600-618.

McCay-Peet, L., & Toms, E. G. (2010). The process of serendipity in knowledge work. *Proceedings of the Third Symposium on Information Interaction in Context.*

McCay-Peet, L., & Toms, E. G. (2015). Investigating serendipity: how it unfolds and what may influence it. *Journal of the Association for Information Science and Technology, 66*(7), 1463-1476.

Mendonça, S., Cunha, M., & Clegg, S. R. (2008). Unsought innovation: serendipity in organizations. Entrepreneurship and Innovation—Organizations, Institutions, Systems and Regions Conference, Copenhagen.

Merton, R. K. (1948). The bearing of empirical research upon the development of social theory. *American Sociological Review, 13*(5), 505-515.

Merton, R. K. (1968). *Social theory and social structure*. Free Press.

Merton, R. K., & Barber, E. (2004). *The travels and adventures of serendipity: a study in sociological semantics and the sociology of science*. Princeton University Press.

Miller, D. (2010). *The book whisperer: Awakening the Inner Reader in Every Child*. John Wiley & Sons.

Monument to Ernest Solvay. (1932). *Nature, 130,* 657.

Munafò, M. R., Nosek, B. A., Bishop, D. V. M., Button, K. S., Chambers, C. D., Percie du Sert, N., ... Ioannidis, J. P. A. (2017). A manifesto for reproducible science. *Nature Human Behaviour, 1,* 0021.

Napier, N., & Vuong, Q. H. (2013). Serendipity as a strategic advantage? In T. Wilkinson (Ed.), *Strategic management in the 21st century* (pp. 175-199). Praeger/ABC-Clio.

Napier, N. K. (2010). *Insight: encouraging Aha! moments for organizational success*. Praeger.

Napier, N. K., Bahnson, P. R., Glen, R., Maille, C. J., Smith, K., & White, H. (2009). When "Aha moments" make all the difference. *Journal of Management Inquiry, 18*(1), 64-76.

Napier, N. K., & Nilsson, M. (2008). *The creative discipline: mastering the art and science of innovation*. Praeger.

Napoli, R. (2021). *The NFT metaverse: building a blockchain world*. Forbes. Retrieved from (accessed on: January 11, 2022) https://www.forbes.com/sites/forbestechcouncil/2021/12/27/the-nft-metaverse-building-a-blockchain-world/?sh=4c5bab5a531c

National Coffee Association USA. (2021). *The history of coffee*. National Coffee Association USA. Retrieved from (December 26, 2021) https://www.ncausa.org/about-coffee/history-of-coffee

Nguyen, M.-H. (2021). Subjective spheres of influence: A perceptual system beyond mindsponge. *PhilArchive*. https://philarchive.org/rec/NGUSSO

Nguyen, M.-H., & Le, T.-T. (2021). Information particle. *OSF Preprints*. https://osf.io/fgjpz

Nguyen, M.-H., Le, T.-T., & Khuc, Q. (2021). Bayesian Mindsponge Framework. *Scholarly Community Encyclopedia*. https://encyclopedia.pub/13852

Nguyen, M.-H., & Vuong, Q.-H. (2021). Evaluation of the Aichi Biodiversity Targets: The international collaboration trilemma in interdisciplinary research. *Pacific Conservation Biology*. Online Early.

Nguyen, M.-H., Le, T.-T., Nguyen, H.-K. T., Ho, M.-T., Nguyen, H. T. T., & Vuong, Q.-H. (2021). Alice in Suicideland: exploring the suicidal ideation mechanism through the sense of connectedness and help-seeking behaviors. *International Journal of Environmental Research and Public Health, 18*(7), 3681.

Nguyen, M.-H., Nguyen, H. T. T., Le, T.-T., Luong, A.-P., & Vuong, Q.-H. (2021). Gender issues in family business research: A bibliometric scoping review. *Journal of Asian Business and Economic Studies, ahead-of-print*.

Nguyen, M.-H., Pham, T.-H., Ho, M.-T., Nguyen, H. T. T., & Vuong, Q.-H. (2021). On the social and conceptual structure of the 50-year research landscape in entrepreneurial finance. *SN Business & Economics, 1*, 2.

Nguyen, H.-K. T., Nguyen, T.-H. T., Ho, M.-T., Ho, M.-T., & Vuong, Q.-H. (2019). Scientific publishing: the point of no return. In Q. H. Vuong & T. Trung (Eds.), *The Vietnamese Social Sciences at a Fork in the Road* (pp. 143-162). De Gruyter.

Pálsdóttir, Á. (2011). Opportunistic discovery of information by elderly Icelanders and their relatives. *Information Research*, *16*(3), 485.

Perianes-Rodriguez, A., Waltman, L., & Van Eck, N. J. (2016). Constructing bibliometric networks: A comparison between full and fractional counting. *Journal of Informetrics*, *10*(4), 1178-1195.

Pham, H.-H., & Ho, T.-T.-H. (2020). Toward a 'new normal' with e-learning in Vietnamese higher education during the post COVID-19 pandemic. *Higher Education Research & Development*, *39*(7), 1327–1331.

Pickering, A. (1992). *Science as practice and culture* (A. Pickering, Ed.). University of Chicago Press.

Popova, M. (2020). *David Whyte on vulnerability, presence, and how we enlarge ourselves by surrendering to the uncontrollable.* Brainpickings. Retrieved from (January 03, 2022) https://www.brainpickings.org/2016/04/11/david-whyte-vulnerability/

Robinson, A. (2020). The archaeology of Armageddon. *Nature*, *578*(7796), 510-512.

Roberts, R. M. (1989). *Serendipity: accidental discoveries in science.* Wiley.

Rogers, J. A. (1972). Darwinism and Social Darwinism. *Journal of the History of Ideas*, *33*(2), 265.

Rosenau, M. J. (1935). Serendipity. *Journal of Bacteriology*, *29*(2), 91-98.

Rubin, V. L., Burkell, J., & Quan-Haase, A. (2011). Facets of serendipity in everyday chance encounters: a grounded theory approach to blog analysis. *Information Research*, *16*(3), 488.

Sampat, B. N. (2012). Mission-oriented biomedical research at the NIH. *Research Policy, 41*(10), 1729-1741.

Satia, P. (2018). *War drove 18th-century Industrial Revolution in Great Britain*. Stanford News. Retrieved from (December 25, 2021) https://news.stanford.edu/2018/05/03/war-drove-18th-century-industrial-revolution-great-britain/

Satia, P. (2019). *Empire of guns: the violent making of the Industrial Revolution*. Stanford University Press.

Schell, D., Wang, M., & Huynh, T. L. D. (2020). This time is indeed different: A study on global market reactions to public health crisis. *Journal of Behavioral and Experimental Finance, 27*, 100349.

Sethna, Z. (2017). Editorial. *Journal of Research in Marketing and Entrepreneurship, 19*(2), 201-206.

Shea, J. J., & Sisk, M. L. (2010). Complex projectile technology and Homo sapiens dispersal into western Eurasia. *PaleoAnthropology, 2010*, 100-122.

Sheng, Z. M., Chertow, D. S., Ambroggio, X., McCall, S., Przygodzki, R. M., Cunningham, R. E., ... Taubenberger, J. K. (2011). Autopsy series of 68 cases dying before and during the 1918 influenza pandemic peak. *Proceedings of the National Academy of Sciences, 108*(39), 16416-16421.

Spencer, H. (2020). *The principles of biology: Volume 1*. Outlook Verlag.

Stahl, M., & Baier, S. (2015). How many molecules does it take to tell a story? Case studies, language, and an epistemic view of medicinal chemistry. *ChemMedChem, 10*(6), 949-956.

Steele, C. M. (1988). The psychology of self-affirmation: Sustaining the integrity of the self. In L. Berkowitz (Ed.), *Advances in experimental social psychology* (Vol. 21, pp. 261-302). Elsevier.

Stengers, I., & Muecke, S. (2018). *Another science is possible: A manifesto for slow science*. John Wiley & Sons.

Stringer, C., Pachitariu, M., Steinmetz, N., Reddy, C. B., Carandini, M., & Harris, K. D. (2019). Spontaneous behaviors drive multidimensional, brainwide activity. *Science, 364*(6437), eaav7893.

Thagard, P., & Croft, D. (1999). Scientific discovery and technological innovation: Ulcers, dinosaur extinction, and the programming language JAVA. In L. Magnani, N. J. Nersessian, & P. Thagard (Eds.), *Model-based reasoning in scientific discovery* (pp. 125-137). Kluwer Academic/Plenum Publishers.

Thanh, V. (2021). *Vietnam PM calls for climate justice at COP26.* VNExpress International. Retrieved from (December 31, 2021) https://e.vnexpress.net/news/news/vietnam-pm-calls-for-climate-justice-at-cop26-4380258.html

Thiem, L.-V. (1949). Über das Umkehrproblem der Wertverteilungslehre. *Commentarii Mathematici Helvetici, 23*(1), 26-49.

Thiem, L.-V. (1950). Sur un problème d'inversion dans la théorie des fonctions méromorphes. *Annales scientifiques de l'É.NS, 3e*(67), 51-98.

Thomas, L. (1956). Reversible collapse of rabbit ears after intravenous papain, and prevention of recovery by cortisone. *The Journal of Experimental Medicine, 104*(2), 245.

Tollefson, J. (2021). Top climate scientists are sceptical that nations will rein in global warming. *Nature, 599*, 22-24.

Toms, E. G. (2000). Understanding and facilitating the browsing of electronic text. *International Journal of Human-Computer Studies, 52*(3), 423-452.

Tuy, H. (1968). On linear inequalities. (English. Russian original). *Soviet Mathematics. Doklady, 9*, 366-369.

Tuy, H. (1986). A General Deterministic Approach to Global Optimization VIA D.C. Programming. In J. B. Hiriart-Urruty (Ed.), *North-Holland Mathematics Studies* (Vol. 129, pp. 273-303). North-Holland.

Tzu, S. (2021). *The art of war*. Vintage.

United Nations. (2021). *Secretary-General calls latest IPCC Climate Report 'code red for humanity', stressing 'irrefutable' evidence of human influence*. United Nations Meetings Coverage and Press Releases. Retrieved from (December 26, 2021) https://www.un.org/press/en/2021/sgsm20847.doc.htm

Uzzell, D. (1999). Education for environmental action in the community: New roles and relationships. *Cambridge Journal of Education, 29*(3), 397-413.

Van Eck, N. J., & Waltman, L. (2014). Visualizing bibliometric networks. In *Measuring scholarly impact* (pp. 285-320). Springer.

Van Kleeck, A., Stahl, S. A., & Bauer, E. B. (2003). *On reading books to children: parents and teachers.* Routledge.

Vietnam Government. (2010). *Decision No. 1483/QD-TTg dated August 17, 2010, of the Prime Minister approving the national key program on mathematics development in the 2010-2020 period*. Viet Nam Government Portal. Retrieved from (March 11, 2021).

Von Clausewitz, C. (2008). *On war*. Princeton University Press.

Vuong, Q. H. (2015). Be rich or don't be sick: estimating Vietnamese patients' risk of falling into destitution. *SpringerPlus, 4*(1), 529.

Vuong, Q.-H. (2018). The (ir)rational consideration of the cost of science in transition economies. *Nature Human Behaviour, 2*, 5.

Vuong, Q.-H. (2019). Breaking barriers in publishing demands a proactive attitude. *Nature Human Behaviour, 3*, 1034.

Vuong, Q.-H. (2020a). From children's literature to sustainability science, and young scientists for a more sustainable Earth. *Journal of Sustainability Education*, 24(3), 1-12. http://www.susted.com/wordpress/content/from-childrens-literature-to-sustainability-science-and-young-scientists-for-a-more-sustainable-earth_2020_12/

Vuong, Q.-H. (2020b). Reform retractions to make them more transparent. *Nature*, *582*, 149.

Vuong, Q.-H. (2021a). The semiconducting principle of monetary and environmental values exchange. *Economics and Business Letters*, *10*(3), 284-290.

Vuong, Q.-H. (2021b). Western monopoly of climate science is creating an eco-deficit culture. *Economy, Land & Climate Insight*. https://elc-insight.org/western-monopoly-of-climate-science-is-creating-an-eco-deficit-culture/

Vuong, Q.-H., La, V.-P., Vuong, T.-T., Ho, M.-T., Nguyen, H.-K. T., Nguyen, V.-H., ... Ho, M.-T. (2018). An open database of productivity in Vietnam's social sciences and humanities for public use. *Scientific Data*, *5*, 180188.

Vuong, Q.-H., Bui, Q.-K., La, V.-P., Vuong, T.-T., Nguyen, V.-H. T., Ho, M.-T., ... Ho, M.-T. (2018). Cultural additivity: behavioural insights from the interaction of Confucianism, Buddhism and Taoism in folktales. *Palgrave Communications*, *4*, 143.

Vuong, Q.-H., Bui, Q.-K., La, V.-P., Vuong, T.-T., Ho, M.-T., Nguyen, H.-K. T., ... Ho, M.-T. (2019). Cultural evolution in Vietnam's early 20th century: a Bayesian networks analysis of Hanoi Franco-Chinese house designs. *Social Sciences & Humanities Open*, *1*(1), 100001.

Vuong, Q.-H., La, V.-P., Nguyen, M.-H., Ho, M.-T., Tran, T., & Ho, M.-T. (2020). Bayesian analysis for social data: a step-by-step protocol and interpretation. *MethodsX, 7,* 100924.

Vuong, Q.-H., Ho, M.-T., Nguyen, H.-K. T., Vuong, T.-T., Tran, T., Hoang, K.-L., ... La, V.-P. (2020). On how religions could accidentally incite lies and violence: folktales as a cultural transmitter. *Palgrave Communications, 6,* 82.

Vuong, Q.-H., Le, T.-T., La, V.-P., Nguyen, T. T. H., Ho, M.-T., Khuc, Q., & Nguyen, M.-H. (2022). Covid-19 vaccines production and societal immunization under the serendipity-mindsponge-3D knowledge management theory and conceptual framework. *Humanities and Social Sciences Communications, 9,* 22.

Vuong, Q.-H., & Napier, N. K. (2015). Acculturation and global mindsponge: an emerging market perspective. *International Journal of Intercultural Relations, 49,* 354-367.

Vuong, Q.-H., Nguyen, M.-H., & Le, T.-T. (2021a). Home scholarly culture, book selection reason, and academic performance: Pathways to book reading interest among secondary school students. *European Journal of Investigation in Health, Psychology and Education, 11*(2), 468-495.

Vuong, Q.-H., Nguyen, M.-H., & Le, T.-T. (2021b). *A mindsponge-based investigation into the psycho-religious mechanism behind suicide attacks.* De Gruyter / Sciendo.

Vuong, Q. H. (2020). The rise of preprints and their value in social sciences and humanities. *Science Editing, 7*(1), 70-72.

Vuong, Q. H., & Napier, N. K. (2014). Making creativity: the value of multiple filters in the innovation process. *International Journal of Transitions and Innovation Systems, 3*(4), 294-327.

Wallas, G. (1926). *The Art of Thought.* Jonathan Cape.

Wang, C., Lu, H., Zhang, J., He, K., & Huan, X. (2016). Macro-process of past plant subsistence from the Upper Paleolithic to Middle Neolithic in China: a quantitative analysis of multi-archaeobotanical data. *PLoS One, 11*(2), e0148136.

Watson, P. (2007). *Ideas: a history of thought and invention, from fire to Freud.* HarperPerennial.

Weiss, E., Kislev, M. E., Simchoni, O., & Nadel, D. (2004). Small-grained wild grasses as staple food at the 23 000-year-old site of Ohalo II, Israel. *Economic Botany, 58,* S125-S134.

Williams, E. N., Soeprapto, E., Like, K., Touradji, P., Hess, S., & Hill, C. E. (1998). Perceptions of serendipity: career paths of prominent academic women in counseling psychology. *Journal of Counseling Psychology, 45*(4), 379.

Yaqub, O. (2018). Serendipity: towards a taxonomy and a theory. *Research Policy, 47*(1), 169-179.

Zhang, Y. C., Séaghdha, D. Ó., Quercia, D., & Jambor, T. (2012). Auralist: introducing serendipity into music recommendation. *Proceedings of the Fifth ACM International Conference on Web Search and Data Mining,* 13-22.

Zupic, I., & Čater, T. (2015). Bibliometric methods in management and organization. *Organizational Research Methods, 18*(3), 429-472.

Index

https://doi.org/10.2478/9788366675865-020

openness · - 27 -, - 28 -, - 114 -, - 117 -, - 122 -, - 123 -, - 150 -

P

Pablo Picasso · - 3 -, - 56 -, - 57 -
Palais du Trocadéro · - 56 -
patent policy · - 20 -
Paul Dirac · - 167 -
Penicillium notatum · - 68 -
perceivable range · - 109 -, - 110 -, - 111 -, - 114 -, - 117 -, - 119 -, - 121 -, - 122 -
personal possessions · - 82 -
pharmaceuticals · - 20 -
Phenikaa University · - 44 -, - 45 -
Picasso's African Period · - 56 -
Plantago asiatica · - 63 -
Plantago major · - 63 -
pneumonia · - 68 -
political power · - 2 -
population · - 3 -, - 76 -, - 83 -
Portrait of Aunt Pepa · - 57 -
Prague · - 65 -
predators · - 1 -, - 3 -, - 68 -
prepared mind · - 24 -, - 28 -, - 29 -, - 30 -, - 115 -
primitive age · - 1 -
pro-serendipity cultures · - 157 -, - 160 -, - 162 -, - 163 -, - 164 -, - 165 -

R

recommender system · - 13 -, - 15 -, - 17 -, - 19 -, - 20 -, - 22 -
reproduction · - 75 -, - 77 -, - 78 -, - 82 -
Robert K. Merton · - 16 -, - 19 -, - 22 -, - 23 -, - 25 -, - 91 -, - 105 -

S

sciences · - 13 -, - 15 -, - 19 -, - 20 -, - 119 -
scientific research · - 46 -, - 55 -
SciMath DB Project · - 198 -
semiconducting principle · - 44 -, - 53 -, - 55 -
serendipity · - 2 -, - 4 -, - 13 -, - 70 -
serendipity relations · - 25 -
sharks · - 77 -
Sisyphus · - 199 -, - 208 -, - 216 -
slow science movement · - 4 -
social stress · - 2 -, - 83 -
social well-being · - 2 -
software · - 14 -, - 20 -
Solvay Business school · - 166 -
Solvay Conference · - 164 -, - 166 -, - 167 -, - 167 -, - 185 -
Solvay Conference on Physics · - 167 -
Solvay Institute of Sociology · - 166 -

T

U